Russell Remembered

Other books by the same author

*The Comforts of Unreason: A Study of the Motives behind
Irrational Thought*
(Routledge, 1947)

*Methods and Criteria of Reasoning: An Inquiry into the
Structure of Controversy*
(Routledge, 1957)

BERTRAND RUSSELL on the terrace at Portmeirion, about 1950

RUPERT CRAWSHAY-WILLIAMS

Russell
Remembered

London
OXFORD UNIVERSITY PRESS
NEW YORK TORONTO
1970

Oxford University Press, Ely House, London W.1

GLASGOW NEW YORK TORONTO MELBOURNE WELLINGTON
CAPE TOWN SALISBURY IBADAN NAIROBI DAR ES SALAAM LUSAKA ADDIS ABABA
BOMBAY CALCUTTA MADRAS KARACHI LAHORE DACCA
KUALA LUMPUR SINGAPORE HONG KONG TOKYO

SBN 19 211197 3

Printed in Great Britain by
W. & J. Mackay & Co Ltd, Chatham

For the whole earth is the sepulchre of famous men; and their story is not graven only on stone over their native earth, but lives on far away, without visible symbol, woven into the stuff of other men's lives.

Pericles's Funeral Speech from Thucydides
translated by Alfred E. Zimmern

Contents

CHAPTER ONE

Russell Encountered

THE Portmeirion Estate lies just north of Harlech on a peninsular between two estuaries. Half-way between the hotel itself and the main road (the drive is about a mile long) there sits a massive pseudo-baronial castle, built in 1840. Clough Williams-Ellis, the creator of Portmeirion, bought the castle sometime in the 1930s and turned it into a separate hotel.

For a year or so until 1934 Bertrand Russell lived and worked there, and in fact wrote *Freedom and Organisation* in the Victorian Gothic Library. When the war began, in 1939, the Castle was taken over by the Ministry of Education as temporary home for a preparatory school from Frinton, which had been evacuated because of the danger of invasion. Owing to the exigencies of war, and with total lack of experience as a teacher, I had come there in 1942 to teach mathematics, French, and English.

In the relatively academic atmosphere of the school the legend of Bertrand Russell's presence was still alive. Indeed there was proof of the legend in the curious diversity and sophistication of the school library. The greater part of the books on the shelves were in fact remnants from Russell's own library (he was then in the U.S.A.) plus many of the books which had been sent to him by hopeful authors and publishers.[1]

The preparatory school moved back to England after the war, and the Castle was turned into flats. My wife and I stayed on in our cottage, which was in what used to be the Castle's stable-yard.

In the late summer of 1945 Amabel Williams-Ellis told us that the Russells were coming to stay at Portmeirion; and she said that

---

[1]'I never read a book after it's published', said Russell once, when swapping boasts. Compare Sidney Smith: 'I never read a book before reviewing it; it prejudices a man so.'

she wanted us to meet them. This was for us the intellectual equivalent of being asked to sit next to the Queen at lunch—an informal lunch, not merely a civic reception or banquet.

I do not think—in retrospect—that this is an exaggeration; nor do I think it would be exaggerated as a description of the feelings of a great many left-minded persons of my generation. Bertrand Russell was, after all, the top man in our field of interest. And to meet someone who is intellectually outstanding—and who is famous for it—is not merely a social/snob pleasure; it is also an undertaking. While one may be impressed by a king, provided one knows the form—the protocol—there is nothing much that can go wrong. With someone like Bertrand Russell, on the other hand, there is always the horrible possibility that the whole conversation may dwindle and disappear into nothing because one is unable to produce a spark of intelligence sufficiently bright to stimulate the eminent brain into action. What is worse, one fears that the eminence may be not merely bored but actively and evidently impatient. And so one feels impelled to try not only to keep the conversation going but also to say something actually worth saying.

By and large, this is of course a mistake. Russell later confirmed that most eminent men, like most ordinary men, prefer gossip and talk about the weather on social occasions to attempts at intellectual fireworks which too often lead to inarticulate embarrassment or half-baked observations on the expert's speciality.

I can still clearly visualize the scene of our actual introduction. It was just inside the front door of the hotel. Russell and his wife Patricia (but she was always called Peter) had just come down the hill from the cottage where they were staying. Russell was smoking his pipe, since he never stopped smoking except to eat or sleep. His wife was looking magnificent: she was extremely good-looking, handsome rather than pretty, with an aquiline nose and striking red hair. Russell's hair was equally striking: long (for those days), abundant, and pure white. (He was vain of his hair, and my wife found that she could tease him by praising the white hair of a gypsy who used to live on the Portmeirion estate. Years later we all much enjoyed the contest between Russell and Frank

Lloyd Wright at a party in a room at Portmeirion, one wall of which is made entirely of looking-glass. Frank Lloyd Wright was so neatly turned out in the American manner that his hair, though less abundant and luxuriant than Russell's, seemed whiter than white.)

I realize now that Russell's white hair must in fact have been on the same level—at the same height—as his wife's red hair; for Russell was not tall. But one never realized this. He always held himself very well, and was without a trace of the quirks which characterize the small man who minds being small. It is amazing how often it happened, during the time we knew him, that people who spent an evening with him simply did not notice that he was comparatively short.

We talked for a few minutes. Then we arranged that the Russells should come up to our house after dinner for coffee. And in the event Russell was of course charming—so charming that one part of my mind, I remember, remained surprised and relieved all the evening. Peter Russell was also charming, and very good company, as she was highly intelligent. But we were not so surprised or potentially awed, partly because she was about the same age as we were.

Russell was as responsive as a hair-trigger in conversation; he listened with concentration to any opinion one put forward, and (most important) his smile instantly encouraged even the mildest attempt to say something amusing. This last is the main ingredient in 'putting people at their ease', and in Russell's case—as probably in most cases—it was motivated in part, I think, by a strong and non-rational desire to please, itself springing perhaps from the effects and memories of his own early uncertainties and anxieties in dealing with the alien world.[1]

Not that the desire to please is the invariable effect of such uncertainties (nor of course am I suggesting that the desire to please

[1] He had been educated by private tutors. His first encounter with young males was at an army crammer's when he was sixteen. The other students were all older than he was; and, as he says in his autobiography (p. 42), 'the most admired among them was a young man who asserted that he had had syphilis and got cured, which gave him great kudos.'

is 'merely' the effect of uncertainty). There seem to be two sharply opposed types of response to anxiety-producing social situations: one type of response shows itself as a wish to please; the other as a wish to be thought *not* to wish to please—a fear of seeming unconfident. Famous men, perhaps because they tend to be pestered by people who like their fame rather than their person, seem more often to react in the second way (or at any rate no one is surprised if they do so). Russell's reaction was most emphatically of the first type. And he himself acknowledged, in later conversation, that his desire to please—to be liked—was extremely strong; it had often made him pull his punches in argument, though only (he insisted) on social occasions, when the consequences were of no account.

On this occasion there was no need to pull punches. We very soon started talking about education. When I had taught in the preparatory school in Deudraeth Castle, the headmaster had encouraged me to experiment in various ways, and especially in allowing the children to be much freer in class than was usual in preparatory schools at that time. I had read enough of Russell's writings on education to know that the popular idea of his views on permissiveness and freedom was an extreme caricature; and I think he was probably relieved to find that he had no need to disclaim such beliefs as that children should never on any account be crossed and that boys and girls should be forcibly mated at puberty.

We soon found that there were many points on which we were in agreement—enthusiastic agreement, in fact, since we were members of what was still in those days a small minority tilting against an entrenched establishment. Partly because of this, and partly because of Russell's charm, that first evening lost all sense of strain within a few minutes. We were establishing what Malinowsky called 'phatic communion', and what Wilfred Trotter described in terms of the 'ritual of herd recognition'. At the time of course we did not break through the surface of the social forms. But some years later, when we were talking about this first meeting, we recognized that a great part of its pleasure for all of us derived from the 'confirmation to one another of our sym-

pathy and of the class or classes to which we belonged', as Trotter
puts it. I had a copy of Trotter's book and I remember I read out
the passage about 'conversation between persons unknown to one
another'. This, says Trotter,

is also—when satisfactory—apt to be rich in the ritual of recognition.
When one hears or takes part in these elaborate evolutions, gingerly
proffering one after another of one's marks of identity, one's views
on the weather, on fresh air and draughts, on the Government and
on uric acid, watching intently for the first low hint of a growl, which
will show one belongs to the wrong pack and must withdraw, it is
impossible not to be reminded of the similar manoeuvres of the dog,
and to be thankful that Nature has provided us with a less direct,
though perhaps a more tedious code.[1]

It was on this later occasion that I asked Russell what he thought
of Trotter's thesis about the herd instinct as a source not only of
undue conformity but also of altruism. Rather surprisingly, considering that he has never referred to Trotter in his writings on
ethics, he said he largely accepted the thesis. Incidentally, it is a
tantalizingly unanswered question whether the Trotter referred
to in the *Autobiography* (Vol. I, p. 114) as wanting a paper from
Russell for the Moral Sciences Club at Cambridge is Wilfred
Trotter. When I asked Russell about it in 1967, he said he could
not remember anything about this Trotter at all.

There was a second reason why that first evening of talk was so
enormously enjoyable for us. It was not merely that we were
establishing Malinowsky's phatic communion; it was also that
Russell's evident desire to make us believe that he was interested
was in itself encouraging and flattering, whether or not it was
just politeness.

As we later discovered, this encouraging attention was due not
only to Russell's desire to please but also to his being sensitive
to the difference in our ages. Although my wife and I were already nearly forty, he himself was nearly forty years yet further
ahead. And therefore, for him, we were so young as to be potentially impatient with the moral and intellectual assumptions of

[1] Wilfred Trotter, *Instincts of the Herd in Peace and War* (London, 1916, revised
ed. 1942), pp. 119-20.

age. Besides, he was still eminent rather than famous: the *History of Western Philosophy* had come out that year in Great Britain, and Russell was only just beginning to notice the fame-making effects of being on the B.B.C.'s television Brains Trust. He had not yet been overwhelmed by undeniable evidence of his prestige.

It was symptomatic of one of his most attractive characteristics that, the next time we diffidently asked the Russells to come and see us, we found that he had been diffident about asking *us* to come and see *them*. It seems on looking back on it, that it took a remarkably short time before our own astonishment that we should be of interest to such an eminent genius ceased to bother us. It was not that our admiration diminished, but rather that the accompanying awe became swamped and overlaid by ordinary affection and friendship. He became primarily not Bertrand Russell, the outstanding intellect, who had so much influenced our early development, but simply, in the present, dear Bertie, to be argued with, laughed with, teased, cosseted, and fed with his favourite foods.

One of the things we talked about that first evening was the problem of introducing children to the technical terms of elementary algebra and geometry. I had been contrasting the old rote-learning method with the more pragmatic method of introducing children first to the objects (the three-sided figures, the four parallel-sided figures, the round-figures, the 'area of field to be found out' etc.) they will have to deal with, and then giving them the names ('triangle' . . . 'x', etc.) as handy devices by which to identify the objects. The pragmatic method is now a commonplace of the New Mathematics; but in those days it was still possible for my predecessor as mathematics teacher to have started children of nine in geometry by writing up on the blackboard a sort of matrix, with the words 'triangle', 'parallelogram', etc., on the horizontals and with their characteristics (three sides, sides parallel, etc.) ticked in the appropriate vertical columns. There were no cut-out models of the triangles, parallelograms, and circles. There were not even any pictures of them. The children just had to learn the matrix by heart, with only the slightest idea of what it was all about.

Russell was suitably horrified to hear all this, though not very surprised, since he knew from his own experience how few teachers realized that the primary qualification for teaching elementary mathematics was not knowledge of mathematics but knowledge of how to teach. He then began to contrast the practical, everyday approach to definition which I was adopting with the logical approach which he had adopted in *Principia Mathematica*. My objective had been simply to make the children associate a name with the object it was normally used to designate. His objective, on the other hand, had been to set mathematics firmly and indubitably upon a base of propositions of pure logic which were themselves rigorously deducible from explicitly stated axioms and rules of procedure.

'How would you introduce children to the definition of the number 2?' asked Russell. 'I imagine you would bring it in quite early in arithmetic?' As he expected, I said that I would bring it in right at the beginning, first by making the child play with pairs of objects and then, when words became appropriate, in terms of adding one and one.

'In *Principia Mathematica*', said Russell, 'the definition of the cardinal number 2 comes at about page 250. And what it says, though in symbols, is: "The cardinal number 2 consists of the class of all couples. These couples are defined as follows: there is some concept or other, which we will call p, such that, if A and B, which are not identical, are both members of p, and there are no other members, then p is a couple." ' I noted a particular satisfaction in his voice when he said this; and we found later that it was characteristic. He took an intellectual autocrat's pleasure in being able to show that things are more complicated or paradoxical than they might appear. He was the high priest endowed with esoteric knowledge; and he had the high priest's temptation to mystify the ordinary man. As we shall see later he sometimes indulged himself so far as to make mysteries grow where none grew before.

Russell did, on this same occasion, produce one of his characteristic paradoxes of argument. We had been talking about the way in which the majority of teachers (outside the middle-class private system of schools) seemed to be socialists, especially since the war. And we were congratulating ourselves on the relative freedom allowed to teachers in Great Britain as compared with the U.S.A. One of us commented on how depressing it must be to feel that you cannot be honest with the children you teach— not even allowed to put both sides of a question, much less your own side.

'It is essential that teachers should be persecuted for their views', said Russell. And for the moment he stopped us in our tracks—as he had intended: we thought we must have misheard, since on the face of it he was going counter to the tenor of our discussion. And of course on the face of it—taking his remark strictly—he was talking nonsense. But if he had said exactly what he meant— if he had talked in terms of the need to prevent atrophy of pro- gressive impulses—there would have been no surprise and in particular no jolt to received ideas.

᪥᪥᪥

Implicit exaggeration was a factor in much of Russell's wit. As he himself acknowledged, it is almost impossible to be funny at the expense of an intelligent person's ideas without being also a little unfair to them. If the ideas are worth bothering with at all, they will seldom be quite obviously foolish. So, in order to make them look foolish enough to be vulnerable to a *concise* (and hence potentially witty or trenchant) comment, they have to be over- simplified in some way. Yet, although Russell acknowledged that his philosophical and ethical arguments often depended for their wit and/or force upon over-simplification, he manifested a curious impenitence about it—curious, at least, if one were being so pedestrian as to consider the probable intellectual con- sequences, but *not* curious when one saw how much fun he got out of it. It was the same kind of fun as one got, when young, out of making up an apple-pie bed. And it was hard—at least in his presence—to prevent any intellectual disapproval one might feel from being overcome by his infectious enjoyment. There was, I think, another reason why Russell was unrepentent. Not only did he enjoy his skill in making up philosophical apple-pie beds. He also had a robust feeling that anyone who could be incapacitated by such booby traps deserved all he got.

A typical example of this kind of philosophical wit occurs in his chapter on John Dewey, the instrumentalist/pragmatist, in *A History of Western Philosophy*. The results, he says, of Dewey's theory of truth are curious:

Suppose somebody says to me: 'Did you have coffee with your breakfast this morning?' If I am an ordinary person, I shall try to remember. But if I am a disciple of Dr. Dewey I shall say: 'Wait a while: I must try two experiments before I can tell you.'

But this (if I may be so pedestrian) is most unfair to Dewey's theory. In the first place, the pragmatic attitude applies to the *verification* or *confirmation* of judgements, not to their original formation. Of course, one will form one's judgement of what one had for breakfast by appealing to one's memory. But if one wishes to confirm that the judgement is correct, one has to start appealing to things one does in the future: such things as searching one's memory further, going to the kitchen and looking at the coffee-pot, asking one's wife, etc. In the second place, the complexities and apparent uncommon-sense aspects of pragmatism derive from its being designed to apply mainly to relatively abstract judgements. This is not to say that Russell's criticism of Dewey's theory of truth was unjustified. It is to say merely that the theory is not so foolish as Russell implied.

Russell was often similarly unfair to the verification principle adopted by logical positivism as a criterion of meaning. But I will leave a discussion of this to Chapter V. I mentioned the Dewey example simply to set an important element in Russell's intellectual scene. I remember on one occasion, when we were discussing Dewey, I said to him 'But that is of course one of your unfair arguments.' 'I *like* being unfair', said Russell. I hope in Chapter V to show not only that he was unfair to Logical Positivism but also that he was unfair to infinity.

We also talked—that first evening—about the widely held belief that Russell refused to use his title. I remember I myself quite took this for granted and had been rather surprised when Amabel Williams-Ellis used the title in introducing him. After all, it was not implausible that he should have renounced the trappings of aristocracy; he was known to be a Socialist, if not a dangerous Bolshevik.

The story was in fact only half true. When he had first inherited the title from his brother in 1931, he had not at once adopted it; and he had of course continued to write as Bertrand Russell. However he had gradually taken to using the title in social contexts. In any case he now saw no compelling reason to give up a title. Like Bernard Shaw, he always distinguished sharply between social and individual morality in such matters. If an individual wished to help those worse off than himself, and if he actually did help them, then he was to be admired. If, on the other hand, he was more concerned—as a Socialist—to try and bring about a social system which guaranteed a minimum living and equal opportunity, then this also was a perfectly tenable view. To be a Socialist committed one to trying to alter the system; it did not commit one to the exercise of private charity, nor to the denial of private comforts. It was therefore a kind of special pleading to claim that Socialists specifically ought to renounce their incomes and advantages. For there is equal obligation on any person, whether right-wing or left-wing, who claims to have the interests of the majority at heart. Strictly speaking all such persons, Russell argued, are ethically obliged to give the top 'tithe' as it were of their incomes to people existing at the lowest level: the value to a Liverpool slum dweller of an extra £1 a week is a hundred times the value of the same £1 per week to a professional man with capital behind him.

It was refreshing to find that Russell was completely down-to-earth about this whole subject. He distinguished clearly between regret and guilt. We could acknowledge an ethical obligation of this sort, and we could also decide with regret that we were not going to act up to it. But, since practically nobody else acted up to it either, this did not entail that we should feel *outstandingly* guilty. We all agreed that no one has any particular right to condemn anybody else on these grounds.

We then discussed the position of someone like Clough Williams-Ellis, who—while remaining a Socialist—owns considerable stretches of land in Snowdonia, besides the Portmeirion Estate. As can be imagined, there were Conservatives in the district, who under the impression that Socialists believe in complete egalitarianism, were shocked by Clough Williams-Ellis's apparent hypocrisy. 'But surely . . .' they would say, 'how can he justify owning so much land? Oughtn't he to give it away or something?' My wife and I had devised an answer to this. And it was nice to be able to tell Russell about it, knowing that he would enjoy it as an atheist and also a friend and admirer of Clough's.

'I'm afraid you've got it wrong', we would say. 'Clough Williams-Ellis is a Socialist. He doesn't pretend to be a *Christian*.'

Russell felt, then, that there was no more obligation upon him than upon anybody else to give away his property to other people. In fact he did give away a lot of money when he was young, and indeed throughout his life. But he did not feel that this was necessitated by his being a Socialist. Analogously, he did not feel under any obligation as a Socialist to stop using a title. What he did feel was that the system of hereditary titles should be abolished; and this was in part because he had none of the currently fashionable illusions about the value of a title. He had no truck with those half-guilty aristocrats who comforted their consciences by saying to each other 'My dear, a title means nothing nowadays!' Russell rather enjoyed his title; and of course he acknowledged that he found it practically useful as a source, in emergency, of privileged treatment in hotels, restaurants, shops, etc.

❧

As is now common knowledge, anyone who knew Russell well called him Bertie. I had first thought, when starting to write this book, that I should for that reason call him Bertie throughout, because this is after all how his friends thought of him.

But unfortunately the name Bertie is a markedly diminutive one. I remember that I was myself illogically surprised when I first realized that this was in fact what he was called by his friends; it seemed almost *lèse-majesté* that anyone so prestigiously eminent should be given such a diminishing name. I also noticed how surprised acquaintances were when they first heard him referred to in this very familiar way; it was as if one were dropping a name with a louder clang than usual.

For this reason my second thought was simply to call him Russell throughout, as is of course done in most biographies. But there are too many awkwardnesses in such a procedure, apart from its stiffness. In the first place, I shall have to refer to my wife —and to some of his wives—by their Christian names. In the second place, it is I am sure significant that he should for the whole of his life have been known by the dimunitive. It cannot be merely the continuation of a childhood custom; it is more probably a symptom of his personality—an expression of his friends' appreciation of the fact that in one small envelope should be contained not only so many of the expected appurtenances of genius but also ordinary weaknesses, incompetences, diffidences so juxtaposed as to make him a person of whom it seemed natural to say '*dear* Bertie'. (His grandmother once to his delight called him 'Dirty Beer'.)

What I have therefore decided to do is to be inconsistent. I have started by calling him Russell, because neither I nor the reader knows him very well as yet. But, in order to give a true picture, I shall in the future alternate the formal and informal styles according to the context.

~~~~~

After this first meeting we saw quite a lot of the Russells, since they were staying for about three weeks at the hotel. But most of our memories of that time derive from rather later meetings, in particular after the Russells had started to do up a house near

Ffestiniog, which we had luckily found for them as it had belonged to the family of a friend who became known to all of us as Henry the Explosion.[1]

However, there was one incident during those first weeks which is typical and relevant. As we were walking down to the hotel one evening, we saw a car with the number FF 7777.

'That's a peculiar number', I said. (I know this is not a very original remark.)

'It's no more unlikely than any of the other numbers here', said Russell crisply. He pointed to the number on another car—some such number as ER 2876. 'The odds against ER 2876 turning up here today are just the same as the odds against FF 7777.'

I saw what he meant; and, on the face of it, it was perfectly correct: the odds against any given number turning up (provided it is within the class of 'accepted car numbers') must be the same as the odds against any other randomly chosen number. But there was something paradoxical here. Somehow, one knew even so that FF 7777 was *much* more unlikely than ER 2876. Russell did not help me. As (I am glad to say) I soon realized, he was deliberately and mischievously misinterpreting my remark. What I had meant, or ought to have meant, was that the number FF 7777 was of an unusual *pattern*. The odds against the appearance of such a patterned number are of course very much greater than those against the appearance of 'ordinary' numbers.

Russell, incidentally, was a confirmed observer of car numbers, and often made up mnemonics for the letters. Our own car at that time, which had the number BPJ 417, was flatteringly identified as a Bloody Potent Jalopy. Russell's years in the U.S.A. had widened his vocabulary.

These years were so important in his life, and in some ways so unpleasant, that one needs to know something about them—and of course about his life in general—in order to see him against the

---

[1] This friend, having the misfortune to crash his powerful motor-bicycle outside the local explosives factory, was the cause of a congregation of ambulances, and the further cause of the widespread inference that there had been a huge explosion in the factory. Russell subsequently talked, in discussing the logical function of proper names, of 'an explosion which we may call Henry'.

right background. I imagine that most readers will already know the basic outlines of Russell's life. I shall therefore do no more here than set the scene by summarizing the events of these American years as they lead up to his return to Britain in 1944.

Shortly before the war, not in order to evade it but because he badly needed to earn some money, Russell went to the United States, first (in 1938) to the University of Chicago as visiting Professor of Philosophy, then in 1939 to the University of California. In 1940 he was appointed Professor of Philosophy at the College of the City of New York. Before he could take up his new position but after he had resigned his chair in California, the appointment was challenged by a tax-payer and was annulled, part of the grounds being—in the opinion of the judge, who was a Roman Catholic—that Russell advocated immoral and salacious doctrines and wrote filth. The judge refused to make Russell himself a party to the proceedings; so he was unable to reply, and the education authority decided not to appeal.

The Faculty of Harvard University, led partly by Whitehead (despite his now disagreeing with Russell's philosophical views), behaved well, and declined to cancel its invitation to Russell to deliver the William James lectures. These lectures formed the basis of *An Inquiry into Meaning and Truth*, which was published in 1940. The British edition displayed on its title page a full list of Russell's academic honours, lectureships, etc., taking up fifteen lines. There was then a space and the words:

> Judicially pronounced unworthy to be Professor of
> Philosophy at the College of the City of New York (1940)

The American publisher was asked to print a similar title page but he refused.

After the Harvard lectures Russell would have been unemployed had it not been that, luckily—as it seemed in the short term—he was offered a job teaching the history of philosophy at an educational foundation in Pennsylvania. The creator and patron of this foundation was Dr. Albert Barnes, an eccentric and wilful millionaire. Russell moved with Peter (Patricia) and his son Conrad to Pennsylvania. But things went badly wrong. Russell developed an acute sinus infection and was temporarily unable to work. Dr. Barnes became hostile, and—in January 1943—dismissed Russell at a moment's notice. Russell sued Barnes for wrongful dismissal and won his case. But it was three years before the money was paid; and in the meantime he was jobless, largely because of the malicious gossip which had been spread after the New York case. However, Russell's years at the Barnes Foundation had the indirect result of solving all his financial problems. On the basis of his lectures he wrote the *History of Western Philosophy*, living in the meantime on an advance from the American publisher and also an advance (on future royalties from books already published) from Stanley Unwin in England.

In 1944 things began to improve. Trinity College made amends by asking him to return as a Fellow and give lectures. The lectures were an enormous success. In America there was published a large symposium on his philosophy in 'The Library of Living Philosophers' series. *The History of Western Philosophy* was published in 1945 in the U.S.A. and 1946 in England, and was an immediate best-seller, with Stanley Unwin unable to get enough paper for the reprints. Money and fame both began to flow. Even then, before he had become world-famous in the context of nuclear disarmament, Russell was the most widely known English thinker, with seventeen books already translated into French and German. He was ten years past normal retiring age, and ahead of him there was a quarter of a century of active work.

It was on this rising tide of success that my wife and I met him.

CHAPTER TWO

1945–8

RUSSELL's series of lectures at Cambridge was due to finish in 1946. He and Peter decided that they would sell their house in Cambridge and buy instead a house somewhere near Portmeirion. When they went back to Cambridge, my wife and I started looking for something suitable, and found—as I have said—a house near Ffestiniog, which is a pretty village 700 feet up in the hills about four miles from the slate-quarrying town of Blaenau Ffestiniog. During most of the year 1946 the Russells were doing up and adding on to the house. It stood 200 yards down the hill from Ffestiniog with one of the finest views in the whole of North Wales, looking across a deep valley to the Moelwyn mountains on the right and westward down the valley to Portmeirion and the sea. It had been the village school in the grounds of the 'big house'. (The big house had been occupied during the war years by A. S. Neill's Summerhill School, a school which was if anything more progressive and rebellious than had been Beacon Hill School.) The school-master's living quarters were attached to the village school itself so that combined they had the ideal shape and form for a servantless era: one very large room, with all the other rooms small and convenient. It was a very sharp pleasure for Russell to be able to let himself go on this house, after the poverty of the years in the U.S.A. The *History of Western Philosophy* was not only bringing in very large sums but also greatly enhancing Russell's earning power as a writer.

In order to be able to supervise the alterations to the house, the Russells spent what time they could up in North Wales, staying either at Portmeirion or at the Pengwern Arms Hotel in Ffestiniog. But even so there were delays—especially, it seemed, when the Russells were not there to make a fuss. Once when they had been unable to get up to Wales for several weeks, the delays seemed unconscionable, and Russell decided that he must make

a protest in person. So he came up just for two nights and stayed
with us.

At dinner on the day he arrived we began talking about the
definition of 'gentleman' which he had delighted us by producing
in a recent B.B.C. Brains Trust. His was the one definition which
eschewed hypocrisy, snobbism, and cliché. Other members of
the Brains Trust had put forward various vague and inconclusive
proposals (such as the one about never being rude except on
purpose). Then Russell said: 'A gentleman is a man whose grandfather had more than £1000 a year.'[1]

'Money talks', we said; and we discussed the confidence and
privilege that money can buy.

'But what about aristocrats?' I asked. 'They have more power
and privilege than anybody.' (Those were the days before expense
accounts had really got going.)

'The point about an aristocrat', Elizabeth (my wife) said, 'is
that he is *not* a gentleman. In fact, he is often a cad.'

We elaborated: we worked out the way in which an aristocrat,
if rich enough and ensconced behind a sufficiently high wall, has
nothing to fear from his neighbours' disapproval. And this im-
perviousness to the neighbourhood is shown in small things as
well as in large things. It is typical of aristocrats that they are
not (or at any rate were not) taught by their nannies to eat everything that was put in front of them, nor were they taught that it
is bad manners to talk about religion and other subjects which
may hurt people's feelings. What is important for them is that
not too many other people should behave as they do.

'The concept of the gentleman', said Russell, 'was invented by
the aristocrats to keep the middle classes in order.'

⁂

Russell had an appointment with the builder and architect at
the Ffestiniog house the next morning. The plan was that we

---

[1] On a later occasion Russell proposed a variant definition: a gentleman is anyone who has a legal right to enter a place marked 'Gentlemen'. He also pointed
out that the House of Lords is the only place which does not rely upon euphemism
for that announcement.

should drive him up in our car. The sun was shining; we had the car open; we began talking philosophy; it was a perfect day. I remember that I asked Russell what he thought of Schiller the pragmatist's *Logic for Use*. When we arrived at the house Russell was halfway through some critical comment. I put the hand-brake on; Russell broke off and said, 'Well, I suppose we'd better go in. Come and back me up'.

Inside the house the architect and the builder were waiting. Russell walked in, said good-morning, and—immediately, without any other preliminaries, without any working up of steam— he boiled over into a furious denunciation of everything that the builder and the architect had done and not done. His face got red, his voice rose an octave, he banged the builder's flimsy table.

'What do you *mean* by this intolerable and quite inexcusable delay?' he roared. 'I have never heard of such incompetence . . .'

The builder and the architect were so taken aback by this eruption that they were speechless for the first few minutes. They went pale with astonishment: their lips trembled.

Eventually the architect recovered himself. 'But, Lord Russell, you are not allowing for our difficulties. We simply could not get hold of the timber . . .'

'That is a *lie*!' said Russell, banging the table once again so that all the pencils and set-squares and boxes of nails bounced and rattled. 'There's no possible excuse.'

Later, the architect tried again: 'Lord Russell; I really do not see why we should take this . . .'

'I don't care *what* you see or don't see . . .'. Russell would hardly allow either of them to finish a sentence. The tirade rolled over them until both of them were left floundering and gasping.

Russell ended off by demanding a complete change in their future behaviour. He stopped talking, and walked smartly out to the car; we got in; I started the engine;

'So Schiller was really making the context of the statement part of its meaning', said Russell.

Elizabeth and I were still stunned.

'But Bertie', we said, 'you seem quite calm!'

'I *am* quite calm', he said. 'That's taught them a lesson I think, hasn't it?'

'We certainly think they were impressed. Do you mean to say', we asked, 'that that whole explosion was deliberate and contrived?'

'Yes indeed', said Russell, 'it was the only thing to do—the only way of making an effect.'

'Well, I suppose it may work', I said. 'But I did think you were being just a little bit unfair at times.'

'Unfair! *Of course* I was being unfair.'

He explained that, whatever he had said, both the builder and the architect would in a few days have persuaded themselves that practically nothing was their fault (since undoubtedly *some* things weren't). If he had been reasonable and had listened to their excuses there would have been nothing gained and no lasting effect at all.

'Perhaps you are right', we said. Then I added: 'But even so, weren't you worried at all about what they would think of you behaving like that? I should have felt—uncomfortable, to say the least, about displaying myself as so much less than reasonable and so far from fair.'

'No, I wasn't worried about that. Why should I be?'

'There you are', I said, 'it's what we were saying last night: you're an aristocrat, and I'm merely a gentleman.'[1]

But it was also, we decided, partly a matter of the generations. Russell had been brought up to feel in his bones that he was superior to 'inferiors'. And his liberal opinions, though they modified his behaviour, were incapable of diminishing his feeling of confident superiority. Whatever the cause of Russell's behaviour, his assessment of the situation was entirely correct. His explosion produced immediate results. Unobtainable wood, non-existent metal, and missing labour appeared like magic, and the Russells were soon installed.

---

[1] A. N. Whitehead once made the same distinction in anger; see Alan Wood, *Bertrand Russell: The Passionate Sceptic* (1957), p. 145.

At this time Arthur and Mamaine Koestler (Mamaine Paget) were living in a converted farm-house about two miles from Ffestiniog. It was on a headland near their house one day that, during a heavily threatening electric storm, we all saw Russell's shock of white hair (and felt our own hair) literally stand on end. It was a frightening moment.

We saw quite a lot of the Koestlers and also of Humphrey Slater, the novelist (known before the war as Hugh Slater), who used frequently to come and stay either with us or in a near-by farm-house. The whole tenor of our political discussions in those days—during the years 1945-7—was conditioned by the fact that Russell and Koestler and Slater together were a powerful anti-communist team. Not only were they formidable as arguers but they also knew what they were talking about. Koestler and Slater had both been members of the Communist Party; Russell had actually 'been there' in 1920 (but he never descended to implying that those who had not been there could not talk) and had become one of the first of the disillusioned.

Like many other left-wing people at that time, my wife and I were anti-anti-communist, partly because we were ignorant of what was going on under Stalin and partly because it was impossible to know how many of the purported facts about the Soviet Union were right-wing propaganda, or wishful thinking. (We remembered the deliberately lying propaganda of the First World War; and in the second there had also been the Russians' cardboard tanks—believed in even by top people in our Foreign Office.) There were of course further factors involved. But this is no place to try and evaluate the whole controversy. The point is that our disagreement with Russell had to be firm and carefully argued (because of the weight of opposition), with the result that it triggered his polemical instincts.

Very soon we found ourselves battling with his convictions. There were two main grounds of dispute: first, the question whether Communism as manifested in Russia was better than Nazism; and secondly, the question whether the Soviets should be let into the secrets of the atom bomb. As with so many of the important questions in a complex world, there were thousands of unknown and unmeasurable factors involved (including social/psychological factors)—so many that no opinion, on either side, could justifiably be held with any certainty.[1] But this of course has never stopped anybody from holding strong opinions. On the contrary, the very fact that there was no way in which opposing views could be tested gave licence, while the very urgency of the issue gave motive, for unbridled convictions.

In the event Russell was as extreme as anybody—a great deal more extreme, indeed, than we had expected. After all, one of the things we had always admired him for was the admirable way in which he had throughout his life combatted his temperamental desire for certainty. And this admiration was confirmed when, in the Introduction to the *History of Western Philosophy*, we found him saying: 'To teach how to live without certainty, and yet without being paralysed by hesitation, is perhaps the chief thing that philosophy, in our age, can still do for those who study it.'

Although none of the autobiographical works had as yet been written, Russell had written a prefatory chapter, 'My Mental Development', for the volume on his work in the 'Library of Living Philosophers' (published in 1944). And it was clear from this essay that his early life had been full of the desire for certain knowledge not merely of mathematical truths but also of matters of fact. He had even, in his twenties, believed in 'the possibility of proving by metaphysics various things about the universe that religious feeling made me think important'. But then he had gradually been forced, by his enquiries, to the conclusion that empirical knowledge—knowledge of matters of fact—could never be more than probable. This had been the pattern of his intellectual life: a passionately metaphysical and idealistic temperament provided the springs of his action; and a ruthlessly efficient intellect restrained its impetuosity and controlled its direction: his temperamental anarchism was constrained into socialism, and his passionate desire to believe into scepticism.

[1] This is a regrettably general point. I shall have occasion to underline it in the future in order to stress that when I question Russell's justification for holding some controversial view with extreme conviction I am *not* implying that my view—or anyone else's—is any better founded.

(*The Passionate Sceptic* was a brilliant title for Alan Wood's biography.) In his writings, where he had time for reflection, the restraint and the controls were properly exercised—at any rate for most of the time. But in live discussion things were often very different.

This had a large influence upon the direction which our discussions took. Both Koestler and Slater felt very strongly about the evil of Soviet Communism; they had after all both experienced the intellectual and moral betrayals of totalitarian expediency. (Koestler himself had carried out such betrayals in the Brown Book of the Nazi Terror; Slater had experienced them as a highly responsible officer in the Spanish Civil War.) But it was Russell who had the strongest feelings of all. This was perhaps partly due to the frustration of having publicly stated, twenty years before in *The Practice and Theory of Bolshevism*, what left-wing people were only just now beginning to acknowledge.

Over the first of the two main questions—whether Communism was worse than Nazism—Russell's behaviour was typically variable. When he was feeling calm, he would simply say that the methods of Communism were as bad as those of any totalitarian state including Nazi Germany. But, when he was provoked—for instance by us, who believed that there was nothing in Russia so bad as the Nazis' concentration camps and extermination—then Russell would often get excited. He would start to say that Russia was far worse than Germany and he would boil over into making large and comprehensive generalizations about 'all Russians'. 'All Russians are imperialists', he would say, for instance, or even, 'All Russians are eastern barbarians.'

When the second question arose—the practical question whether the Soviets should be given the secrets of atomic energy—the generalizations became yet fiercer, partly perhaps because supremely important practical decisions were involved. Russell was convinced that the Russians would steal our secrets and keep their own; they could never be trusted, he said; it was not just that they would fail to keep their word; their treachery was deliberate and as it were constitutional. Elizabeth and I found that we could not accept such dogmatism without protest. We felt that, even if

Russell were right in his general attitude (and I acknowledge of course that he turned out to be much more right than we were), he simply had not got sufficient evidence to justify such large *and* extreme generalizations. There is after all a valid distinction in this context between being sure you are right and being sure on good grounds that you are right. But the only result of our protesting was that Russell was goaded into yet wilder assertions. He once managed even to say that *all* Russians would 'crawl on their bellies to betray their friends'.

Russell himself would have argued—and did—that it was sensible as a matter of expediency for him to be extreme in his expression of his views. He claimed, in the *Autobiography*, (Vol. I, p. 63) as characteristic of himself 'the practice of describing things which one finds almost unendurable in such a repulsive manner as to cause others to share one's fury'. This practice may well have worked sometimes, especially in confirming the convictions of the already converted, and also sometimes in attracting the young uncommitted idealist. For it remains true—despite all Russell's own efforts to prevent it—that great strength of feeling is widely regarded as a sort of guarantee of certainty and probity. (The obverse is the belief that a man of moderate opinions is a weakling.) Moreover, even if one disagreed with what Russell was saying, there was something extraordinarily attractive and persuasive about the vigour, the single-heartedness, and the sincerity of his enthusiasm, heightened as it was by his assumption that naturally all right-thinking people and all nice people agreed with him.[1]

But the chief factor in encouraging Russell to such extremes of statement was that with Koestler and Slater, both expert supporters, he felt himself to be intellectually 'among friends' in a rather special sense. I think a large part of the secret of Russell's polemical energy and influence lay in this habit of relaxing his scepticism among friends. The battle to curb with rational scepticism

[1] He exercised the same persuasiveness in talking philosophy. Many philosophical theories depend upon the initial acceptance of arbitrary assumptions about the proper meanings of words, such as 'know' in epistemology and 'ethics' in ethics. Russell was particularly adept, as I explain later, in forcing one to accept the necessary assumptions without noticing that one was being so forced.

his emotional desire for certainty must always have been a strain.
An occasional release of vigilance was essential. (As one of us
remarked it was hardly surprising that when Russell let his hair
down, there was rather a lot.)

But one cannot relax one's standard of caution except in the
presence of people who will implicitly accept that there are unstated reservations attached to one's broad generalizations. Russell
himself, I remember, once said to me 'You will never get a
democratic government to work in Africa.' And he followed this
up with a whole list of the respects in which democracy is too
inefficient to carry out its own plans in a time of crisis. Here he
was relaxing his scepticisms in order to give rein to his basic
anarchism. And, if I had not been in the mood to argue, that
would simply have been a rather wild generalization which I
would have accepted with the usual reservations (among convinced democrats) about democracy being the least of the evils.
But of course if Russell had not known me to be on the same side
he would have framed his generalization much more cautiously.

As it happens, on this occasion I queried the generalization. I
said there might be a danger of democracy failing, but many
Africans must still feel it was worth trying; I suggested we could
very soon find enough people with experience of government
but without the will to power; and so on. And of course Russell
then modified the simplicity of his assertion: he started discussing
seriously how much weight it should be given, how it applied to
Kenya and so on. There were innumerable other occasions of this
sort. What one got in practice was a most effective combination:
on the one hand, Russell felt free to go to extremes when talking
with friends, since they knew what reservations were implied; on
the other hand, there was the valuable check of a sceptical brain
efficiently used. This meant that it did no harm that the reservations were so to speak temporarily in abeyance. For they could be
forced into the open if necessary.

But, even though the reservations would be acknowledged if
the occasion should arise, the very fact that they were not explicit
allowed Russell to attach extreme conviction and approval or
(more often) disapproval to his generalizations; and the result

was that he would often continue to *feel* in extremes even when he had withdrawn to a more moderate and intellectually defensible position

This happened typically over Soviet Communism in 1947-8, and later over such controversial issues as nuclear disarmament, civil defence against nuclear war, the Kennedy assassination, etc. And it later happened sometimes over people's motives. Russell would indulge his wish to feel that the issue was clear by assuming that only fools or knaves could possibly disagree with him. As most of his friends were in his opinion not fools, the ones who disagreed with him were temporarily knaves. But more of this later.

It was this superstructure of extreme feeling on a rational basis which gave Russell his force and influence as a polemicist. It is after all a truism that the entirely reasonable man, whose opinions are not convictions, will seldom get things done. The courses of action that he advises may be right, but they are not carried out. In this sense Russell was not an entirely reasonable man. He was a man of passion and action. All the same, he was by no means the *ordinary* excitable man. The great difference between him and most polemicists was that he could usually be pulled back from his extreme position, and indeed he would often come back of his own accord when seriousness was in order. His basic sanity had in fact devised an effective kind of 'strategic arguing' which operated a defence in depth of his more cherished opinions.

When he was in active mood and relaxing his scepticism, he would feel free to rally his spirits and those of his comrades-in-arms. He would advance far forward, and take up an apparently dominant position. This after all is what most of us do: we are led on by the yessing of our friends, by not being exposed to carping criticism; we do not therefore notice the evidence mounted against us; we stand on a commanding height above it. Then, having persuaded ourselves that our position is impregnable, we try to hold on to it. And when we find after all that it is vulnerable we lose our tempers.

This is where Russell differed from other people. Most of us conform to Oscar Wilde's defininition of man as 'a rational animal who always loses his temper when called upon to act in accordance with the dictates of reason'. Russell did of course sometimes get furious. But the point about his argumentative strategy at its most effective was that he recognized an untenable position—and also (perhaps this was the aristocrat in him) did not mind losing face. Directly an untenable position was attacked he abandoned it, retreated, and rearranged his forces. He would then acknowledge that the forward position had been untenable. This continually happened; it was one of his most remarkable attributes; and it was connected with his—again remarkable—ability to accept evidence against what he believed. (Not that he always did so, of course. The point is that most people never do so.)

But, although on most subjects Russell was able to combine highly coloured feeling with penny-plain judgement, there have been a number of periods in his life during which one subject has dominated his emotions, and has generated in him such extremes of feeling that the judgement was inevitably affected. In such cases it was not merely that he was unduly certain of his judgement; it was also that the judgement itself tended to be distorted. This is of course only my opinion. There are many people who would say that Russell was often especially right when he was most extreme.

At this time (1947–8), it was about Soviet Russia that he was extreme. (In the late 1960s it was of course Vietnam.) And, as I learnt from Miles Malleson on the occasion of Russell's ninety-fifth birthday party, the anti-Soviet feeling in the 1920s was even more intense than it was in 1947. (But this may have been because Miles Malleson himself was a great deal more pro-Communist in the 1920s than my wife and I were in 1947, and may therefore have provoked Russell more.)

It was in 1947 that there arose the question whether the Soviet Union should be coerced by the threat of atomic weapons. As is now well known, Russell was at that time in favour of such coercion. But he was the victim, both then and later, of the Fallacy of Extension: his views were extended far beyond what he actually said. His position is clear from a letter to *The Times*

of 30 November 1948, in which he referred to misrepresentations
of an address he had recently given at Westminster School, and
stressed that he had urged not 'immediate war with Russia' but
that 'the democracies should be *prepared* to use force if necessary,
and their readiness to do so should be made perfectly clear to
Russia'; and finally he did not exclude 'military means if Russia
continues to refuse all compromise'.

It seemed to us that on this question Russell's judgement had
both a rational and non-rational component. The rational component was the quite serious and arguable view that the only hope
for the human race in the atomic (as it was then) age was international control of atomic weapons, and the only hope of this
in its turn was world hegemony under one power. It is perfectly
true, as Russell later asserted, that his main motive was the avoid-
ance of the chaos of an atomic war. Indeed, he argued at the time,
I remember, that hegemony even under an authoritarian power
would be preferable. If the positions had been reversed, and it
had been Russia which alone had the atomic bomb, he would,
he said, have advocated hegemony under Russia, though with
great reluctance. However, in the conditions of the time, with
America dominant, it had to be the other way round. And, as it
happened, this was the way Russell's feelings preferred.

Elizabeth and I took the somewhat negative view in this case
that such a course of (possible) action could be justified only if it
were almost dead certain to attain its end; that is, successfully to
coerce the Russians into accepting American dominance. This
raised the whole question of ends and means; and we went on to
discuss the received idea that what is wrong with Communism
is that it makes the end justify the means. We were all in agreement
that this was nonsense. Bertie referred to an occasion when he
had been discussing ethics on a wireless programme with Lord
Samuel. Samuel had just made the conventional claim that to
make the end justify the means is wrong. Bertie had said, 'What
else could justify the means?!'

What was wrong with Communism (we agreed) was not that
it made the end justify the means but that it was too certain both
that its (bad) means would attain the (good) end and that the

good of the end outbalanced the bad of the means. *If* one could be highly certain (say) that the killing of kulaks would bring about a highly desirable classless state, then the killing might perhaps be justified. But the Communist leaders could never conceivably have been sufficiently certain of this.

Elizabeth and I argued that if these considerations applied to the Communist 'means', then they ought to apply also to America's threat of the atom bomb. Russell's counter-argument was that the threat alone would probably suffice and that in any case the issues at stake were so enormous that a large risk must be taken. Although this is a perfectly arguable view, it was also of course the view which satisfied Russell's emotions. It is probably significant that, when Patrick Blackett brought out his book on *The Military and Political Consequences of Atomic Energy* in 1948, Russell strongly objected to its general thesis, which was—broadly speaking—that 'the dropping of the atomic bombs on Japan was not so much the last military act of the Second World War, as the first act of the cold diplomatic war with Russia'.[1] Russell claimed at the time that there was evidence available in our Embassy in Washington to support the official view of the motives for dropping the bomb.

Here again his view was tenable. The point, however, was that in discussing such questions the fervour of Russell's advocacy was multiplied ten-fold by his hatred of Soviet Russia. This meant that 95 per cent of his opinion was as it were a function of the feeling against Russia. When this feeling was finally suppressed, the memory of the opinion itself was also suppressed. It is this, I think, which explains the—at first sight astonishing—lapse of memory in the 1950s, when he flatly and furiously denied having ever 'supported a preventive war against Russia'.[2] Later, he acknowledged that he had in fact advocated the use of threats and (in a television interview with John Freeman in 1959) that

[1] Or, as James Byrnes, the U.S. Secretary of State, put it (according to the physicist Leo Szilard) early in June 1945: 'The bomb was needed not to defeat Japan but rather to make Russia more manageable in Europe.' See *Command Decisions*, ed. K. R. Greenfield (London, 1960), p. 402. There seems to have been a lot of confirming evidence of this view.

[2] See *The Nation*, 17 October 1953.

'of course you can't threaten unless you're prepared to have your bluff called'. But, when he was denying it all, he was impregnably dogmatic. Elizabeth and I found it quite impossible to do more than make tentative hints like 'But I seem to remember that you thought we should at least threaten the Russians.'

'Never; that's just an invention of a Communist journalist!' he would say; and we knew that, although we could perhaps query particular points, we could not seriously pursue the general subject without badly damaging our friendship. So we were pusillanimous. This certainly seems to be not simply a case of (negative) forgetting; it was a powerful and positive repression of unwelcome sentiments, with the associated judgements repressed at the same time. Russell himself in referring to his denials said:[1]

I had, in fact, completely forgotten that I had ever thought a policy of threat involving possible war desirable. In 1958 Mr. Alfred Kohlberg and Mr. Walter W. Marseille brought to my notice things which I said in 1947, and I read these with amazement. I have no excuse to offer.

Perhaps it is underlining the obvious to say that with this last short sentence as a pendant the whole complex incident epitomizes an aspect of Russell's genius: his emotional absorption in a 'cause' was all or nothing yet he could withstand the temptation to rationalize his errors.

༼ᘛ ᘚ༽

I do not want to give the impression that our first years of knowing Russell were full of disputation. It is true that we talked probably more politics than do most people, at any rate when Koestler or Slater were present (owing to their bitterness and strength of feeling). But in most ways and at most times it was a period of completely delightful intellectual exploration for me. Although at first Elizabeth and I both felt extremely respectful, and although I was philosophically a lay admirer with no

[1] In a comment on a letter in the *Listener* of 28 May 1959.

technical knowledge, it was as I have said surprisingly soon that we all felt completely relaxed together. This was due in part to Bertie Russell's own character (he was such a very unformidable genius) and to Peter Russell's friendliness. But it was also largely because on *all* other questions we were fundamentally in agreement. And so most of our early conversations combined discoveries of agreement about ends (very heart-warming when one already feels a strong liking) with discussions about ways of attaining these agreed ends (very exhilarating).

I still have a large index card on which I worked out our scores on a questionnaire designed to act as an indicator of left-wing/right-wing attitudes not only in the political field but in all fields. This was the Wisconsin Scale of Radicalism and Conservatism which was used by Sheldon in his work on the psychology of constitutional differences.[1] On this scale there are twenty questions divided into four 'conscious areas' and marked from 1 for extreme conservatism to 5 for extreme radicalism. The total score of an extreme conservative would thus be 20, and of an extreme radical 100.

The total scores of all four of us, including Peter Russell, were all within a mark or two of 85. This overall agreement applied also in detail. In the religious 'area' we all scored the full 25! The only reason why the scores were not more radical was that the scale itself had been devised in the 1920s, and left-wing opinion in Great Britain had changed on such questions as the sacredness of the family and observance of the law. The notion of the sacredness of the family had been a powerful bastion of the *status quo*, and hence it had been a target for Marxist propaganda in the 1920s and 30s. (Russell himself had been very doubtful about it.) But by 1946, partly perhaps because of the psychologists' emphasis on children's need for love and security, the family had become respectable in the eyes of the Left. Again, in the 1920s left-wing people felt that the ruling classes had a stranglehold which could not be broken by constitutional methods. But by 1946 this view had greatly changed, at least in Great Britain. Russell's view at that time was that the democratic process was

[1] W. H. Sheldon, *The Varieties of Temperament* (New York, 1945), pp. 491 ff.

infinitely valuable as a safeguard, however inefficient it might be in other ways. It must therefore always be preferred except in the rare cases where practically *all* 'right-thinking people' (i.e. sincere believers in democracy) are agreed that only by by-passing it can an intolerable situation be remedied.

CVVVVO

We gave Russell quite a little battery of tests of various sorts at this time. I had used a number of I.Q. and aptitude tests when I was teaching during the war. I also had the apparatus for an American aptitude test called the Wiggly Block, which was designed to in-dicate ability to think in three dimensions rather than two.[1] We found for instance that Clough Williams-Ellis—an architect—did well, while his wife Amabel—a writer—did badly.

Bertie Russell did very badly.

'There you are', we said, 'you haven't got a three-dimensional mind. You'd have been no good as a motor-car designer . . . Perhaps you could have been a painter?'

'No', said Bertie, 'I've got a one-dimensional mind.'

And of course he was right. Mathematical logic consists almost entirely of linear deductive sequences; no analogies, no shooting off in different directions after empirical hypotheses. We then asked him about chess, which is a sort of two-dimensional de-duction, and he said he had never been particularly good at it.

Not only had Bertie a one-dimensional mind; he also had *par excellence* a verbal (as opposed to visual) imagination. For him reality was mediated in symbols; in many situations there was no grasp of what was going on except via the medium of words. His need for verbal symbolization was dramatically shown when I gave him an I.Q. test of the analogies type—the type which shows, at its simplest (say) a single-lined circle next to a single-lined square, and then shows by itself a double-lined circle and expects

[1] It was a wooden cuboid, about a foot long and eight inches across which had been divided long-ways into three times three long segments cut in 'wiggles' all of which were slightly different in the amount of curve, so that there was only one difficult-to-work-out way of fitting them together.

the testee to pick out from various alternative shapes a double-lined square.

At first Bertie was much faster than any of my pupils at the school had been. This was extraordinary because the innate intellectual ability primarily measured by such tests does not appreciably increase after the age of sixteen and because in practice people tend to get worse at such tests as they get older. We got quite excited. And then, to our surprise, Bertie gave up before he got to the end.

'Please can I stop now?' he said, 'I can't do them.'

We tried to make him go on, but he obviously hated the idea too much; it would have been boorish to try and force him.

'But what went wrong?' we asked. 'You were doing so well up to then; and the people who do well on the early questions invariably do relatively well on the more difficult questions.'

'I hadn't got any names for the shapes', said Bertie.

And this indeed was the explanation. At the beginning of the test the shapes were quite simple: circles, diamonds, rhomboids, undecagons. So Bertie was able to verbalize the problem: 'as two arcuate undecagons are to three wiggly rhomboids . . .'. But as he got near the end, the shapes became so many and so complex that there were no reasonably concise descriptive names available. From that moment his apprehension of the shapes failed. (Of course there was probably another factor in his refusal to go on. At his age and eminence there was very little competitive intellectual impulse in him. He already knew after all that his I.Q. was quite high.)

Many years later he had another and quite different reason for not wanting to bother with a problem. It was in January 1959, when the B.B.C.'s *To-night* programme posed the brilliantly difficult problem of how to identify, with only three weighings in a balance, a non-standard penny among twelve pennies. I put this to Bertie partly out of curiosity, to see whether his mathematico-logical mind would find it easy. But he refused even to listen to it. He said, 'No, I don't want to do a problem like that. All that will happen is that I shan't solve it, and my mind will buzz for two days.'

He then told us that Herbert Spencer had suffered greatly from
over-activity of the brain. He (Spencer) always went to dinner
parties with two ear-plugs in his pocket. If the conversation got
too stimulating, he put the ear-plugs in his ears and remained
silent for the rest of the evening.

Bertie was, in fact, almost a caricature of the unpractical
philosopher, and the idea that he should actually know what to
do in a domestic/mechanical emergency was laughable. Once,
when he was staying with us on his own, Elizabeth and I both
had to be out at four o'clock. And four o'clock was the time that
Bertie simply had to have his tea; without it he was miserable.
Elizabeth tried to explain to him exactly what to do. But he said
he would never be able to remember any instructions. So she
prepared everything very carefully: the tea in the tea-pot, cup
and saucer ready, the kettle filled. Then she wrote out the instructions in chalk on the slate table in the kitchen:

Lift up the bolster of the Esse (cooker); move kettle on to hot-plate;
wait for it to boil; pour water from kettle into tea-pot; . . . and so on.

When we came back at five o'clock Bertie was miserable and
the tea was still unmade.

CVXXXXV

Bertie's practical disabilities were paralleled by a sort of practical discomfort in some social contexts. It was not that he was incompetent in such contexts. On the contrary, his upbringing had
forced him to 'learn the rules'. He was remarkably good at being
polite: he was a flattering guest and a thoughtful host; and his
manners were so old-fashionedly perfect that he could not sit down
at a party if there were women standing. (This meant, incidentally,
that drinks parties became tiring for him in his nineties unless
they were so small that everybody could sit down.) It was all
the more endearing, then, to find that he could, on occasion, be
overcome with a bashful silence. I remember, very early on, our
all going into a chemist's shop because he wanted to buy a comb.

The assistant waited enquiringly; there was a pause; finally Bertie said to me in a low voice, '*You* ask'.

There was also an occasion when his daughter Kate, who lived in the U.S.A. and whom he had not seen for about twelve years, was coming to stay at Portmeirion with her husband Charles Tait. At the time Bertie was staying with us, and we had arranged that Kate and her husband should walk up to our house for tea after settling in at the hotel. We all three went out in the car that afternoon and for some reason were late back. We began to be worried about the possibility that the Taits might have already arrived at our house and found no one there. And sure enough, as we came up the drive we saw in the distance a man and woman standing on the left of the road by the bend outside our house. 'Oh dear', we said, 'they've found the house empty and come away again. What a horrid welcome!'

The car was open and we were all sitting in the front, with Bertie near the door. I drove smartly up to the couple, stopped beside them and smiled apologetically, waiting for Bertie to greet them.

There was silence. They began to look puzzled.

Then Bertie turned to Elizabeth and me and said in a loud whisper: 'It isn't them!'

⁓⁓⁓

The car I had then was an American two-seater convertible with the impressive name Essex Terraplane and a 'dickie'—a boot in the form of a seat which opened up and took two people on their own in the fresh air and rain. Like any man who has enthusiastically and successfully pursued women all his life, Bertie did not want to admit a term to the pursuit. And, in any case, he was twenty or thirty years younger than his chronological age. Sometimes, therefore, he would leap into the dickie to keep some pretty woman company. But even a fifty-year-old may slip while making such a leap. And at first we made the mistake of being worried more for him than for the woman.

In fact, he was as agile, then and for many years after, as a gazelle. The only occasions when his youthful energy seemed to be really dangerous were when walking in rocky and mountainous country. He always wore conventional town clothes, wherever he was; and these included not only a waist-coat even in the hottest weather but also thin smooth leather-soled shoes (partly because they were more comfortable than heavy country shoes). We suffered perhaps unnecessary agonies when watching him on dangerous ground; for such shoes would have been a handicap even to a gazelle. There were several desperate afternoons on the grassy slopes of a high point near Aberdaron. Bertie walked and talked nonchalantly on these slopes. But they were very steep and they ended with a seventy foot sheer drop into the sea. I spent a lot of time trying unobtrusively to get myself just below Bertie, though I suppose the only result if he had slipped would have been that we would both have perished.

From the time that we first met Bertie Russell I have occasionally made diary or journal entries of incidents which seemed amusing or interesting. At the beginning this was only on rare occasions and purely for my own pleasure. But as time went on the entries became more frequent and acquired a partly Boswellian intent. I told Bertie that I was Boswellizing him, and he was pleased.

I propose to include some of these journal entries, without preamble; some do not have specific dates. The first such entry, for example, might refer to any time between 1947 and 1950.

Take Bertie and Peter and Conrad to Nant Pasgan. Marvellous spring day. Lunch outside. Bertie and Conrad go up Moel Ysgyfarnogod before lunch. Conrad lingers behind on the way down. We ring the ship's bell for him at lunchtime but he still does not appear. We ring it again and he does eventually arrive about half-an-hour late. As he comes into ear-shot he says: 'I didn't hear the bell the first time.'

Conrad obviously enjoyed his own skill in pronouncing Ysgyfarnogod. He is the perfect intellectual's son; enormous and cherished vocabulary.

[Nant Pasgan was (and is) Elizabeth's 'country house'—a well-found cottage, once farmhouse, in an isolated valley 800 feet up in the mountains. Conrad, Bertie and Peter's son, was about nine or ten years old. Moel Ysgyfarnogod is 2045 feet.]

Conrad's intellectual vitality made him very quick in picking up new information and new ideas. On another occasion when we were all at Nant Pasgan we began talking about the well-known experiment in which a pike is put into a large tank with some minnows. The pike attacks and eats the minnows. Then a glass plate is put into the tank so as to divide it into two halves, and a new lot of minnows is put into the half where the pike is not. The pike at once starts to attack, but every time he bumps into the glass plate. In due course he gives up attacking at all. Finally, the dividing glass plate is taken away, and the minnows are again freely available. But the poor pike does nothing; he has learnt his lesson.

Conrad got the whole theory of conditioning in one. 'The minnows had stopped being eatables and had become bump-me-noses', he said.

A few months later, in London, the Russells' spaniel Beauty bumped into the glass door at the entrance to a shop. When Conrad then opened the door for her she delighted him by very sensibly refusing to budge.

∽◯᷌᷌᷌◯∽

At tea yesterday, one of us remembered the Clerihew:

> Huntley and Palmer
> Grew calmer and calmer.
> When either felt restive
> He ate a digestive.

'Can't we produce some others?' said Elizabeth, 'What about Peek Frean?'

> 'When they couldn't be seen,
> They ate a Peek Frean.'

said Bertie at once.

> 'But their *most* secret vice', said Elizabeth,
> 'Was McVitie and Price'.

⌇⌇⌇⌇⌇

Sitting over tea today Bertie told us how on his last journey by
train to London, he had been recognized by an Ancient Mariner
of a fellow-passenger, and talked at non-stop until, unable to get
a word in edgeways and almost fainting with boredom, he was
considering whether or not to pull the communication cord.

'I have an idea', Elizabeth said. 'The next time this happens
you say at once "Well, no, as a matter of fact I am *not* Bertrand
Russell, although I am often mistaken for him. But I *do* admire
him more than anyone in the world. I can count his virtues
from here to Paddington. He is the most wonderful . . ." '

Bertie took up the thread. Sitting up straight in his chair as
though in a railway carriage, he began in a loud platform voice:

'BERTRAND RUSSELL, Sir, is by FAR the cleverest man on
earth. There is no one to touch him, he is hard-working,
abstemious . . .'

We all began to contribute:

'I flatter myself, Sir, that I do one good deed a day, but
Bertrand Russell does ten.'

'I am no mean performer myself in matters of manual dexterity,
but Bertrand Russell could pick the lock on the crown jewels
with a hairpin.'

'I make a good cup of tea if I say so myself—but oh you
should taste Bertrand Russell's!'

'As you can see, my friend, I have a good head of hair myself,
but compared to Bertrand Russell; I am bald, he has 200 hairs to
every one of mine.

On we went, in mounting absurdities, by this time almost
helpless with laughter.

'Good, better, best, bertie.'

'Lotts Road Power Station can smoke, but look at Bertie!'

'Canute failed, but watch Bertie!'

'Yes, indeed', said Bertie, wiping his eyes. 'Canute was a silly
fellow. I shall command the waves to carry on as usual.'

It was a lovely afternoon, full of the feeling of exhausted well-being which is the aftermath of helpless laughing. For hours afterwards even the word 'Bertie' was enough to set us off again.

Bertie's laughter, when he really let himself go, was very characteristic and very difficult to describe. He would take his pipe out of his mouth—to prepare himself as it were for the opening of his lungs. Then he would make a very loud noise for a very long time—pause—sigh—and say 'Oh my! Oh my!'

⟡⟡⟡⟡

Today, when we were having tea, there was a heavy thunderstorm. For some reason Elizabeth went to open the sitting-room door, immediately above which was fixed a telephone junction box. At the same instant this junction box was struck (or at any rate attacked in some way or other) by lightning. There was a piercing and high-pitched bang, and blue flames appeared around Elizabeth's feet. Since she was clearly quite unharmed, Bertie and I resumed our conversation. Elizabeth, still in the grip of her remarkable experience, became restive at our lack of excitement. 'Goodness', she eventually interrupted, 'you two are going on as though nothing had *happened*.' 'Oh', said Bertie, removing his pipe and observing her over the top of his spectacles, 'I see; I think I know what's wrong. How's this: OOOOOh . . . you might have been *killed*; what a *narrow* escape. And my! how brave you were! What consummate courage! Anybody else would have . . .' For a moment words failed him; it was indeed difficult to think how a coward's behaviour would have differed from Elizabeth's when faced with so instant a danger. '. . . would have had hysterics—demanded a doctor and a specialist—and a lightning expert . . .'

'Thank you', said Elizabeth. 'That was *exactly* what I needed.'

⟡⟡⟡⟡

As the Wisconsin scale of radicalism confirmed, everything was fundamentally harmonious between the Russells and us, apart from the disagreement about Soviet Communism, which in any case involved a particular matter of policy rather than a general principle. In philosophy our discussions were I think especially enjoyable on both sides: on my side because I was learning academic philosophy from the most stimulating and authoritative source imaginable, and on Russell's side because he enjoyed teaching, in informal and undemanding circumstances, somebody who was already on the right lines—who was clearly a disciple in matters of principle and of ethics (empiricist, physicalist, sceptic, utilitarian), and who was eager to learn.

There were also several lucky pieces of timing, which helped to make Russell feel that I might be an unembarrassing disciple.

First, just before meeting him I had had an article published in a journal called *Polemic* which was being edited by Humphrey Slater. The article critically examined an argument of Russell's about the existence of universals which he had put forward in his *Enquiry into Meaning and Truth*. Humphrey Slater had sent this article to Russell—before I met him—suggesting that he might like to answer it in *Polemic* himself (which he did).

The second piece of lucky timing was that my book *The Comforts of Unreason* was soon to be published by Kegan Paul (very respectable). The third piece of luck was enormous. There was a plan that the book should be reviewed on the B.B.C. Third Programme. So the B.B.C. people, who knew that Russell was staying at Portmeirion, asked me whether I thought there was any point in asking *him* to review it. I thought there might be, as, although he had not yet seen a copy of the book, he had seen one chapter which had been printed in *Polemic* and also of course he had seen the article on universals.

I did ask him, feeling—as can be imagined—extremely diffident; and he said Yes at once, with his nicest smile. What a marvellous moment that was—for a writer with his first book just burgeoning! I still remember it with pleasure and gratitude.

CHAPTER THREE

A Need for Reassurance

WHEN I say that I was an eager learner of academic philosophy it is literally true that I was a learner. I had read practically no philosophy at all; I did not even know what are the 'problems of philosophy'. But I fairly soon picked up enough of the assumptions and technical terms of philosophy to be able not merely to learn from Russell but also to discuss at least some points with him and with Freddie Ayer, who came to stay several times when Russell was here. I mention Russell's teaching and my learning in order to set the scene of our meetings during the next few years. The point is that I learnt enough for it to be possible for us to discuss in detail Russell's first, and in effect only, draft of his book on *Human Knowledge* (which was published in 1948) and also later to discuss most of *My Philosophical Development* (eventually published in 1959).

The usual routine was that, when Russell had finished a chapter or two of *Human Knowledge*, he would come down from the Ffestiniog house by bus, with us fetching him from the main road (there was petrol rationing still), and we would then have a session of two or three hours. I would read the typescript aloud to Bertie and Elizabeth; and it was understood that anybody could interrupt to comment.

During the first sessions I took it for granted that the *whole* object of the exercise was critical philosophical discussion; and, although I naturally felt that neither Elizabeth nor I had any authority for serious criticism, I did assume that our comments could be useful at least in pointing to passages which were too difficult for the layman or in clearing up ambiguities.[1] And I

[1] *Human Knowledge* was aimed ostensibly at the layman, though I think the aim was in fact wildly out: the book was a discussion of the highly technical Problem of Knowledge—which has no relevance to the layman's problems in actually gaining useful empirical knowledge. (See Chapter V).

also assumed that Elizabeth and I could bring up any points on which we needed instruction. Accordingly, in the first sessions I would sit down with Bertie's typescript on my knee, and coffee or a drink by my side; and—before starting to read—I would perhaps raise again some point we had discussed last time, or would talk in general terms about philosophy. Even if I did not thus delay reading I would sometimes take an opportunity offered in the first pages of raising a new point for discussion.

As I have said, Bertie's manners were always perfect. So the only indication I had that something was amiss came from a certain tenseness and brevity in his comments on what I said— a tenseness which wore off after we had read half-a-dozen or so pages. Sometimes it was accompanied by a quiet tapping of the knee. I do not know how quick I would have been to spot the trouble if it had not been that at some of these sessions it was my turn to read something which *I* had written either as an exercise in academic philosophy to be criticized by Bertie or as a working out of some of my own ideas. I noticed that I got a distinct and quite intrinsic pleasure in reading aloud what I myself had written; and realized that the pleasure might be even greater if someone else were reading it aloud to me.

This, then, was perhaps the trouble! Bertie was impatient because he wanted a good satisfying dose of this pleasure, like a first drink, at the outset of the session. When he had had his drink he was happy and relaxed, and was able to discuss things at any length we all wanted.

Incidentally, Bertie invariably drank whisky and water when he came for drinks; he wanted precisely two fairly strong whiskys in an evening and he asked me to give him no more; for, he said, he found the two drinks gave him the optimum desire and ability to talk. We always had lots of beautiful Scotch Whisky even in those days of shortage; for a Scottish distillery sent a case every month to 'The Earl Russell' with its respectful compliments. Bertie never looked this gift horse in the mouth; for he feared that it might be meant really for his brother.

Bertie's good manners made his tenseness at the beginning of our reading sessions almost undetectable except to people who saw him day by day. Indeed his manners were highly efficient at the task of concealing his motives. He had one very ingenious trick which he used with a certain brisk expediency for cutting short that kind of domestic discussion which can sometimes elaborate itself into a self-indulgent moiling over of pros and cons—whether one should try and get back money paid to a garage for an incompetent repair, for instance, or whether one should have a party this week-end when the Joneses unfortunately won't be here rather than next week-end when the Joneses will be here but everybody else will have had enough of parties.

On such occasions Bertie would usually join in for some time, even if he were not himself concerned. But then we noticed a peculiar thing. While we were still arguing, with no decision in sight, Bertie would suddenly come out with an absolutely definite judgement. It was as if he were a computer which had been working away upon the information fed into it, and which had finally produced its solution.

'It's perfectly clear', he would say, 'we must have the party this week-end.'

'Oh; do you really think so?'

'Yes; no doubt about it at all!'

And then he would start talking about something else.

This device often worked. We were persuaded into acquiescence by the force of his conviction, as one is persuaded into optimism by people who emphatically state that the rain will have cleared off by lunchtime. But then we gradually realized that these decisions were quite arbitrary. Their sole purpose was to stop the discussion. And Bertie simply came down on the side which lent itself most conveniently to a firm and concise judgement.

∽⧼⧽⧽⧽∾

I hope no one will think that, in these pages, I am accusing Bertie of an excessive vanity. As he himself realized most clearly, *all* authors have an enlarged vanity. He was delighted with a remark which I found attributed in a novel to Logan Pearsall Smith:[1]

---

[1] Although it sounds very genuine, I have not managed to verify its source. Bertie himself did not remember it. The novel was *One Man's Poison* by Sebastian

'Every author, however modest, keeps an outrageous vanity chained like a madman within the padded cell of his breast.'

Perhaps—it is at least arguable—Bertie's vanity may have been greater than some people's. But the picture is complicated by the fact that the vanity was gradually overlaid by a concomitant of what was I think modesty and uncertainty. And the picture is further complicated and also confused by the fact that both the vanity and the uncertainty manifested themselves in an apparent desire to be praised.

While Bertie was actually writing *Human Knowledge* the desire for praise was little more than the normal writer's desire for encouragement. And it showed in predictable ways. It was very important, for instance, that I should find an opportunity at least two or three times in a session of saying how impressed I was not merely by the conclusions of some argument but in particular by the cogency with which it was presented.

What was so enjoyable about these sessions was that there was no need for hypocrisy. There was always a sufficiency of cogent arguments and of wit and humour. But although there was no shortage of things to praise, there was still needed some little effort. For it meant a continual search of one's vocabulary for varied but not too inappropriate aspects of enthusiasm.

If sometimes I failed in this Bertie would begin diffidently to fish. 'I rather like that bit', he would say. Or 'Do you think that point is sufficiently clear?'

Human Knowledge was published in 1948; and, although it was reviewed very widely, it did not have the kind of reviews that Bertie was hoping for. (I will try and explain why in Chapter V.) His marriage broke up in 1949, and Peter went off to live in Cornwall, taking Conrad with her. The immediate result of the break-up was that we saw a great deal of Bertie and we learnt to

---

Fox, published about 1956. Unfortunately one cannot ask the author, as 'Sebastian Fox' was apparently a pseudonym for Gerald Bullett.

know him in a way which had been impossible before. This was partly because Bertie's upbringing had prohibited any discussion of his more private life while his marriage persisted; and it was partly also an indirect result of his having made over the Ffestiniog house to Peter. He now hoped to be able to use it and eventually to buy it from her, since she was not going to use it herself. And in fact when she put it on the market in 1950, he commissioned me to try and buy it for him, as he was then on a lecture tour in Australia. But Peter sold it to Professor Michael Postan, the economic historian.

Although this was unfortunate for Bertie it was of course very nice for us; for it meant that when he came to North Wales he stayed with us instead of at Ffestiniog. And I think it may have been in some ways nice for him also. There were naturally stresses and strains after the break-up of the marriage which needed to be relieved and catharsized in talk. And in any case it was a very depressing time for Bertie, finding himself alone at the age of seventy-eight, and with disappointments in his work. (Even the great popular success of the Reith Lectures on *Authority and the Individual* did not altogether please him. There must be something wrong with his argument, he felt, if practically all his critics and correspondents agreed with him!)

Certainly—and I am sure that this was largely because Elizabeth and I were so unmistakeably fond of him—Bertie soon began to relax in the way one does with friends who, one knows, will put up with one's unthinking reflections and undisciplined enthus- iasms—or irritations.

There are few greater pleasures than the early stages in such a friendship, when one is finding that it is more and more safe to relax. I vividly remember a particular walk in the Gwyllt (the woods attached to Portmeirion full of azaleas and rhodo- dendrons); it was a sunny spring day and we ended up sitting on a grassy slope, looking down on the beach. For some time Bertie aired one of his own long repressed irritations. Then it was our turn to do the same with our own current irritation—in this case one of those irritations which has to be repressed because it is occasioned by a friend who is in other respects much too valuable to risk losing. Finally, just before we started back home, we were suddenly able to say how much we were enjoying ourselves and to acknowledge that this was partly because we were being more uncharitable about our friends than would normally be considered quite nice.

But in addition to these pleasures there was the fact that Bertie never seemed to have off-days, as other people do. Even when he was talking about his own miseries he preserved a sense of proportion, an astringency, a willingness—should occasion warrant—to be witty or amused in parenthesis, so that he was *always* good company. It is very nice to think that in that time of loneliness and uncertainty Elizabeth and I were able in return to do something for him which he felt to be valuable.[1]

As Bertie gradually relaxed with us, it became more and more clear that his uncertainties were coming to the fore, and that he had in fact a powerful and profound need for reassurance not only about the intellectual aspects of his life, but also about the personal aspects. It is possible, as I have said, that Bertie's vanity and his modesty (or desire for reassurance, or however one likes to characterize it) were greater than those of most men. But, if so, it was only because the emotional, as well as the intellectual, scale of all Bertie's attributes was that of a genius. Indeed it is a cliché that what makes a man of inordinate achievements is often a set of inordinate drives. Bertie's drives were tremendous: he certainly

---

[1] And it was nice also that he told us this. I quote from a letter he wrote to me in September 1949 just before he went on his lecture tour of Australia. It was enclosed with a sort of memorandum giving detailed requirements and suggestions for the final piecing together of the first two volumes of his *Autobiography*, in case I became responsible for its publication. (I was then—and until his fourth marriage—his literary executor.) He stressed that the object of the *Autobiography* was to make money. Then he ended up by saying—

> When I die my MSS should be sold quickly, before I am forgotten. I have many.
>
> I can't express how grateful I am to you and Elizabeth for your friendship and interest in me. It has made all the difference to me this summer, when I might otherwise have sunk into a black despair.
>
> yrs ever BR

(How inconceivable it was then that the MSS, documents, etc. should fetch hundreds of thousands of pounds!)

had a powerful and nagging desire to persuade other people of his opinions, and he had an equally powerful desire to induce in other people his own emotions. During the first years that we knew Bertie, however, none of these impulses was particularly marked. It was only after his marriage with Peter had broken up, and after *Human Knowledge* was published, that a desire for re-assurance became urgent and almost painful; and what he needed to be reassured about was mainly his power to 'make the world a better place' by influencing other people's minds and hearts.

There was also some need for reassurance in the personal field. However, it was relatively easy for us to help here. Although Bertie's sense of personal inadequacy was non-rational and there-fore by its nature not amenable to cure by rational persuasions, this did not matter. For the only cure we could offer was itself not rational: the spontaneous administration of simple affection.

In the intellectual field it was very much more difficult to help. The reviews of *Human Knowledge* had been disappointing in that, although they acknowledged Russell as being one of the great philosophers and were therefore on the whole appropriately re-spectful,[1] they did not treat the thesis as relevant to current philo-sophical enquiries, much less as the definitive solution of the Problem of Knowledge which Russell himself felt it to be.

I had been able to be quite sincere in my agreement with the main arguments of the book while we were reading it; and I was therefore also able to be sincere in talking about the value of the book as a contribution to philosophy. (It was only gradually that I gained the confidence to question some of the assumptions which Russell, in common with other philosophers, took for granted.) This was very lucky. For neither Elizabeth nor I at first took

[1] There was only one, that I remember, which was markedly disrespectful. That was Stephen Toulmin's review, for the layman, in the *New Statesman*. There was also a somewhat unpleasant notice in the *Philosophical Review* for January 1950 by Norman Malcolm, which characterized Russell's style as 'jaunty and bouncy . . . the patter of a conjurer' and which accused him of slap-dash, slip-shod language. Russell was annoyed by Toulmin's review but upset by Malcolm's; he was sufficiently sensitive about it to ask me to try and find out why Malcolm had sent him an offprint; he felt that it must have been meant unkindly. (I assume—perhaps wrongly—that it was simply a matter of academic convention, since Malcolm knew Russell personally.)

Bertie's need seriously. We simply could not believe that anyone so guaranteedly worthy of his eminence could possibly entertain any self-doubts. So at first we kept missing our cues and made no particular effort to stress our valuation both of *Human Knowledge* and of Bertie's influence on the minds of men in general. However, since our valuation was in fact very favourable, *rapport* was not fractured. We soon came to realize how much, at that moment, Bertie needed encouragement.

Even so, we were astonished at the sheer extent of his demand— probably more so than is the present reader, if he has read the second volume of the *Autobiography*. In the early part of this volume, covering the years of the 1914–18 war, there are a number of very revealing letters to Ottoline Morrell and Constance Malleson (Colette). We did not see these letters when we read the autobiography in 1949, and so we had no idea how extremely confused Bertie had been in those years about his own nature. The letters make it clear that despite his scepticism he had the most oddly metaphysical feelings about his emotions and impulses. 'The centre of me is always and eternally a terrible pain . . .' he writes to Colette in 1916, '—a searching for something beyond what the world contains, something transfigured and infinite . . . —it's like passionate love for a ghost.' (Bertie told us once that he had written masses of extremely purple passages in his early twenties, and had destroyed them all.) In the letters to Ottoline Morrell he is continually concerned by the conflict between his two temperaments—between the metaphysics and the scepticism: 'There *must* be something more important [than this world], one feels, though I don't *believe* there is.' And of course he is also continually worried by the conflict between the pragmatic need for socialist planning of priorities and the idealistic love of freedom. He knows in his head that without socialist planning you get freedom only for the middle and upper classes; yet his bones feel differently. He does not like 'the spirit of Socialism'. Similarly with the conflict between material and spiritual values. Writing from Soviet Russia he says: 'I cannot give that importance to man's merely animal needs that is given here by those in power.' But then he at once acknowledges the counter-argument: 'No doubt that is because I have not spent half my life in hunger and want as many of them have.'

It seems possible that the metaphysical caste of these conflicts and confusions was in part a product of sexual frustration in early manhood. Once a metaphysical essence has been distilled out of repressed sexual energy, it may well remain for years afterwards imbued with the pleasurable associations of the satisfactions for which it stood proxy, even after these satisfactions have been directly achieved.

The confusions of his nature were certainly a worry to Bertie. The feelings of insufficiency to which they led were not merely intellectual; they were also moral and social. Even after years of knowing Ottoline Morrell he tells her he is always paralysed with terror in her presence. He is troubled by a Sense of Sin with capital letters. And he despairs of ever doing any fundamental work in philosophy.

Of course, as he admitted, there can be a kind of vanity or conceit involved in such self-abnegation. In the same way as shyness is sometimes a product of fear of not making the best of oneself—of not being taken at one's own valuation—so a feeling of insufficiency will sometimes be a product of disappointed ambitions; and the self-abnegation may therefore be a kind of attempt to disarm criticism in advance (a sin well known in theological circles).

Any attempt to speculate in this way about the hidden causes of Bertie's anxieties will be misunderstood unless it is seen as complementary to, rather than contradictory of, the straightforward view that Bertie's feelings were genuinely modest feelings of insufficiency.[1] As feelings go, they were certainly what one would normally call modest, in contrast to feelings which

---

[1] I need to stress this point in order to guard against the 'merely fallacy'—what Julian Huxley has called Nothing-buttery. The traditional attitude towards this kind of explanation is that it 'explains away' the modesty by claiming that it is 'nothing but' disguised vanity. This attitude is a result of what I have elsewhere called the Universal Context Assumption: that is, the assumption that if, for example, what appears to be altruistic behaviour is correctly described in any context as (say) a product of childhood guilts, then it is a product of childhood guilts in all contexts—as it were absolutely. This is of course a mistake. It may well

one would call boastful or conceited. At the same time there was as I have said also an appearance of what would normally be called vanity. This I think was a result, not of Bertie's undue conceit, but of the calibre of his intellect and actual attainments. He was far too clear-headed and free of false modesty not to recognize his own position; and his hopes and ambitions were consequently set much higher than those of lesser men. Most people with feelings of insufficiency are anxious to be reassured that they have some modicum of human worth. But this was not true of Bertie. He was not frightened of being thought negligible. It was merely that he hoped he was perhaps one of the two or three greatest and most influential intellects of our century. (This ambition, after all, was as appropriate in Bertie's case as (say) the ambition of a lesser man to be acclaimed a leading figure in his town or country.) Of course this hope was not formulated in any positive or explicit way. Nevertheless there was a corner in his mind which cherished the possibility that it might indeed be justified.

At the time of the actual reading of *Human Knowledge* none of this emerged at all clearly. The reassurance he wanted then was in relation to his writing and his wit. But, later, after the disappointing reception of *Human Knowledge*, Bertie became greatly concerned as to his effect upon the moral and intellectual climate of opinion—his social significance. Often he would ask straight out whether we thought some book had had a considerable influence. Did we think that the implicit injunctions of *The Conquest of Happiness*, for example, had really had an effect on young people at the time? As far as we ourselves were concerned, we

---

be that the altruistic man's motives for his nice actions are as selfish as those of the nasty man for his nasty actions. It remains true, though, that the altruistic man's actions *are* nice and that they need to be contrasted in everyday contexts with those of the nasty man by being called 'altruistic'.

In fact, we need to differentiate in the field of human psychology between the evaluations of people's behaviour towards other people which are appropriate to everyday contexts and those which are appropriate to the more esoteric contexts in which we work out problems of causation, responsibility, deterrence, therapy, etc. Behaviour which needs to be thought of in these esoteric contexts as a product of selfish impulses or of disguised vanity may still be quite correctly thought of in everyday contexts as unselfish and modest.

were easily able to confirm his hopes. I had come from a liberal/ atheist family. So Russell's views were welcome as overt rejection of traditional morality and conservatism. Elizabeth, who had rebelled against the traditional ideas of her family and milieu, was powerfully fortified in her rebellion by the discovery that, far from being alone, she was in eminent and patently rational company.

Although there may not have been many people who were actually converted by Russell's arguments, this was hardly his fault; there are few people who are converted by *any* arguments after the age of majority. On the other hand I think there must have been thousands who were encouraged and fortified in the same way as were Elizabeth and I. I remember being impressed by the warmth of gratitude which Boyd Neel, the conductor, still felt (and expressed when he came to stay at Portmeirion) for Russell even after thirty years. His whole intellectual development had been transformed as he grew up, by the discovery that his doubts about traditional morality were neither unique nor necessarily wicked.

It was not too difficult, then, for Elizabeth and me to reassure Bertie about his beneficent influence in what one might call the social sector of the intellectual field. There remained, however, the purely philosophical sector. The trouble with Bertie's uncertainties and disappointments over *Human Knowledge* was that they were neither imaginary nor inflated. The book was indeed being valued at a much lower level than he had hoped.

CHAPTER FOUR

1948–53

IN 1948 Russell very nearly died as a result of accepting an invitation from my uncle (Sir) Laurence (Collier) who was at that time Ambassador to Norway. Collier felt it would do the Norwegians a lot of good to listen to Bertrand Russell. So he suggested to the British Council that they should arrange for Russell to give some lectures in Norway. We told Bertie we thought he would like Laurence Collier; so he arranged to stay at the Embassy rather than in a hotel under the auspices of the British Council.

Collier expressed some of his reasons for inviting Russell in a letter written after the visit had been arranged. He said, in part:

Russell has a great reputation here and I have hopes that his visit will have a considerable effect both generally and on the narrower political front.

I know that Russell is not primarily concerned with international politics; but I felt . . . that it was time to introduce influential Norwegians to a vigorous and intelligent exponent of Western European ideals who was determinedly opposed to Communism and, indeed, to any form of totalitarianism for reasons transcending either Conservative or Socialist politics. Here, as elsewhere, convinced opponents of Communism and of Moscow policy tend too often to be either men of the Right whose political philosophy, when they have any, shades off into something not far removed from Fascism, or dyed-in-the-wool Labour politicians and trade union bosses who object to Communism as a rival to their own systems of control for the people; and between these elements the large section of the public which is comparatively reasonable, open-minded and tolerant finds itself lost and uncertain, though I think it feels instinctively that it ought to do something to resist this new threat to human values and is ready enough to be mobilized if the fundamental issues are put clearly before it.

That is what I personally hope that Russell may do something to bring about; and I am letting you know this in case you should have an opportunity of saying so to him.

The lectures were a great success. 'He is, as you say, very good value', Collier wrote, 'he gave an excellent lecture last night (in Oslo) to a record audience from the anglo-norse society, very much on the lines which I had hoped for, and is to give two more here to other bodies.'

The first lecture was to have been at Trondheim. Bertie flew up from Oslo on 2 October in a flying boat. The weather was stormy, with heavy rain and a gale of wind. Just as the sea-plane touched the water on arrival at Trondheim, a gust of wind blew it on to its side and let the water in.

'There was a violent jerk', said Bertie in a letter to us, re-counting the episode (the present account is pieced together from several letters),

and I found myself on the floor with some inches of water in which hats, coats, etc. were floating. I exclaimed 'Well, well!' and started looking for my hat, which I failed to find. At first I thought a wave had broken in at a window; it didn't occur to me that it was serious. I was in the very back of the plane, the only part where one could smoke; this turned out to be the best place to be. After a few minutes the crew opened a door and got the passengers from the back through to an open window, and shoved us one by one into the sea. By this time their haste had made me realize things were serious. I jumped clutching my attaché case, but had to let go of it to swim. When I got into the water I saw there was a boat close by. We swam to it and were pulled aboard. When I looked round nothing was visible except the tip of a wing. The swim was about 20 yards. I saw nothing of what happened at the other end of the plane; I imagined they jumped through another window. I gather the people killed were stunned when the accident happened. One of them was a professor concerned in arrangements about my lecture. I pointed out my float-ing attaché case to the people on the boat, and last night a policeman brought it. The things in it were all right, except that the silly books [thrillers] were somewhat damaged. No other piece of luggage was rescued.

The people who had come to the airport to meet me were very solicitous, and drove me at breakneck speed to the hotel. . . .

Then came the usual avalanche of journalists, including one who asked Russell whether he had thought about mysticism and

logic while in the water. (Russell said what he had thought was
that the water was cold.)

'I was not brave, only stupid', Bertie commented. 'I had always
thought a sea-plane would float. I did not realize there was danger,
and was mainly concerned to save my attaché case . . .'

Bertie was none the worse for his immersion. The only things
that suffered were the thrillers in the attaché case, and his trousers.
Peter Russell went to Bertie's tailor a few days later to order a
new pair.

'I'm afraid his present trousers are rather damaged,' she said.

'I am not surprised', said the tailor in a disapproving voice, 'I
understand his Lordship has been *swimming* in them!'

Bertie got on very well with my uncle Laurence, who had a
large fund of Edwardian and Foreign Office jokes to swap with
Bertie's Victorian ones. Here is part of a letter which Bertie wrote
to Elizabeth on his return:

I was glad you were impressed by the profundity of my reflections
while in the water. My time in Norway was very agreeable: I loved
both the people and the country. Now I am off to Berlin, which will
be less agreeable but more interesting. . . . I liked Rupert's uncle. We
had a polite discussion as to who should go through doors first; when
we reached the Embassy he insisted on my going first, saying 'I don't
believe in this Elevation of the Host.'

⁓

Sometime in May 1947, in the middle of all his worries about
his influence on the world, Bertie gave a broadcast in a series on
'What I Believe'. He had a post-bag of seventy or eighty letters.

Bertie sent me, as a present, the whole file of letters, saying they
might interest me 'as they give a picture of average sentiment in
England at the present time', and he added: 'The one that gave me
the most pleasure was the one saying that Satan inspired my talk.'

I still treasure the file as a documentation of idiocy. (But it was
not of course a representative picture.) The letter about Satan
which pleased Bertie began: 'What a truly horrible talk you gave
last night—one which was energized by Satan. In all his traps, he

always puts *some* good bait, otherwise he would not catch any victims.' Another letter began: 'Dear Sir, Having listened with interest to your talk on the wireless last night, I am writing to say how much I pity you.'

I find that I have included in my file of letters to Bertie one or two odd letters of later date. There is an American who writes in 1961 with a plan of salvation and the proposal to 'drop you a letter about once a fortnight and will be pleased to hear from you in turn'. And another American—an advertising man—says that his business is based 'on a philosophical concept of the relativity of matter, energy and its absolute opposite of eternity, spirit, emotion, God or whatever you choose to call the dimension that is mathematically the opposite to time.'

There is also a Canadian, writing twice in August 1958 from Toronto with a large brush pen to 'Mr. Bertrand Russell, Wales, U.K.', enclosing first a press photograph of Princess Margaret, marked 'Good Riddance', and secondly the large block capital message: ALL WELSH SCOTCH IRISH & BRITISH ARE DRUNKEN, UNPROGRESSIVE FLAG-WAVING BAST-ARDS. But the most strongly felt is perhaps a post-card ad-dressed to Bigot Russell, and with again a large printed message: YOU ARE A VERITABLE **NINCOMPOOP** AND YOUR SLIMY, FILTHY, IGNORANT SOUL WILL EVENTUALLY DISCOVER THAT FACT WHEN YOU AND (OTHER STINKERS) ARE BURIED **IN HELL** FOR ALL **ETERNITY**. **REPENT!**

In addition to these polemical kinds of letter, Bertie has always received a surprising number of requests for information or help. Sometimes they are rather naïve. I have a letter from a Mr. Davies, marked in Peter Russell's writing 'An example of the sort of thing I answer ten times a day!' 'Dear Sirs, (it says) just a line to ask you please have you a book on "What politics has done for Wales" in Welsh please and oblige.' Even this was outdone one evening when the Russells were in their Ffestiniog house. There was a knock on the front door at about nine o'clock. Bertie went to the door and opened it. Outside there was a farmer from up the hills.

'I have come, Lord Russell', he said, 'to ask you to explain the theory of relativity in one sentence.'

⌒∨≷≷≷⌒

If the response to the 'What I Believe' broadcast was a some-what feeble reassurance for Bertie, at least there was the O.M. the next year. We knew that he very much wanted the O.M.; it was an honour on a different scale from anything else. And he had been disappointed not to get it earlier. On the other hand, he had been consoled to note that it was always the 'soupy' people who were the first to receive such honours. (We used the word 'soupy' to characterize opinions and temperaments which came down on the supernatural side, not merely in the religious field but in all fields: anti-determinist, for instance, in history and biography; believing in vitalism and Mind; in innate wickedness, in Absolute and eternal verities; and so on.) The soupy are after all pillars of the Establishment; and it was only to be expected that people such as Jeans and Eddington and Whitehead should be regarded as more respectable than Russell.

Bertie came up to stay with us a few days after the award was announced; so we gave an O.M. party for him in the Garden Room at Portmeirion. Among those at the party was the much beloved Elena Gerhardt, one of the greatest of *lieder* singers, naïve, transparent, and sincere, who would boast innocently and un-self-consciously about her audiences and how they acclaimed her. When we introduced her to Bertie she said, with all the graciousness and charm of the *prima donna*: 'You will not have heard of me, Lord Russell. But I have admired and honoured you for many years. May I congratulate you . . .' I do not think she intended her first sentence to be taken *au sérieux*; but it was true.

Bertie's liking for music was genuine but not urgent. I don't think he ever felt an active need for it except when in the com-pany of some woman who loved music herself and whom he loved—or hoped to love.

This must I think have been the first year that Elena Gerhardt had returned to Portmeirion since the death of her charming and admirable husband, Fritz Kohl. Partly in order to keep herself occupied, she was writing her autobiography. And, like Bertie, she would come up to our house at intervals and read us the latest instalment. One day there was some mistake in timing, and at the front gate of our courtyard there appeared simultaneously Elena Gerhardt and Bertrand Russell, each with a little attaché case full of autobiography. As can I hope be understood, and in spite of our veneration for both authors, we found this delicate situation quite irresistibly comic, particularly since both their attaché cases looked identical.

Although Bertie did not actively need music, he was very happy to listen to it in company. He and Peter used often to come up from the hotel after dinner for coffee and music and talk. Bertie and Clough (Williams-Ellis) were both very fond of the old Nadia Boulanger set of Monteverdi madrigals, and especially of *Zeffiro torna*, with its two intertwining tenors. Our cottage has, as a garden, a sort of courtyard with mown grass and very high walls round it. We have large loudspeakers on wheels which can be moved out into the courtyard; and, owing to the walls, we are able to have music out of doors at night without upsetting our neighbours. Some of our pleasantest memories are of sitting on the lawn with Bertie and Peter and Clough and Amabel and listening to these tenor voices coming softly out of the darkness, rising up when they sing of the mountains, and dipping down when they sing of the valleys.

When Patrick Blackett was awarded his Nobel Prize for physics in 1948 he had not yet met Bertrand Russell. This was not so surprising as one might think. Patrick Blackett is by temperament a sceptical empiricist, and the extreme opposite of a 'philosopher'.[1]

---

[1] I should perhaps explain here, since it will be relevant in the next chapter as well, that I have proposed (in 'Two Intellectual Temperaments', *Question*, 1, Feb. 1968) a distinction between on the one hand the 'philosopher', whose temperament wants to find out what things are 'really'—what is their True Nature— and on the other hand the 'empiricist', who is primarily concerned to find out how things should be treated for specific purposes. Thus the empiricist finds out

As a consequence, he had not moved at all in philosophical/
speculative/intellectual circles. However with Blackett only a few
miles away (the Blacketts had, and have, a cottage on Clough
Williams-Ellis's estate near Plas Brondanw) it seemed obvious
that the Blacketts and Russell should meet. So we fixed that the
Blacketts should come to tea one day when Russell was staying in
Ffestiniog. And we also asked Jack and Margaret Huntingdon
(Margaret Lane), who had already met the Russells and who then
had a holiday cottage near Deudraeth Castle.

Bertie arrived a little before the others; and we took the opportunity of showing him a long article about him in some
American paper, which we had been sent that morning by Margaret Chapman (Storm Jameson) with her compliments to
Bertie, in case he had not seen it. It was in fact news to Bertie.
So we spread it out for him on the kitchen table. 'What a *lot*
about me!' said Bertie, licking his lips. And he settled himself
down to read. About five minutes later the Blacketts and the
Huntingdons arrived simultaneously. They took off their coats
and then we led them through into the kitchen. As we all stood in
the kitchen doorway, with me prepared to do the introductions,
Bertie rather reluctantly paused in the middle of his reading—
but without lifting his eyes from the paper—and said: 'I'm very
sorry; I cannot pay attention to anybody. I am *reading about
myself.*'

～⁓⁂⁓～

When Bertie got the Nobel Prize, we wrote to congratulate
him. Here is his reply:

---

about glass, for instance, that it needs to be treated as solid for everyday purposes
but as liquid for the purpose of calculating the effects of long-term pressure.
And he is content with this. But the philosopher wants more; he wants to know
what glass is *really*: is it solid or is it liquid? And similarly with such questions as
whether our wills are free, whether machines can think, whether learning is a
continuous or discontinuous process, whether altruistic actions are self-interested
(as in the discussion a few pages back) and so on indefinitely.

41, Queens Road,
Richmond, Surrey.
3.12.50

Dear Rupert and Elizabeth,

Thank you for your letter. The money, as you say, is nice. I try to think I like the honour equally, but I don't. I have to go to Sweden this week to get the prize but I shall be back on the 12th. Soon after that I hope I shall be able to come to Wales.

America was beastly—The Republicans are as wicked as they are stupid, which is saying a great deal. I told everybody I was finding it interesting to study the atmosphere of a police state, which didn't make me popular except with the young.

When I get back from Stockholm I propose to retire from the world, give up globe-trotting & take to writing. I think the 3rd. world war will begin next May. It seems too late to fuss about this century. Much love—BR.

The visit to America which he mentioned in this letter brought about what was by far the most important thing to happen to him in these years. This was his meeting—or rather re-meeting—with Edith Finch, who was to become his fourth wife. During his visit to U.S.A. they saw each other in New York. She had been for years in love with him; he fell in love with her; and everything was perfect. He brought her down to stay with us, when she later came over to England. We were absolutely delighted with her and happy for Bertie.

But it is not for me to try and say what has been better and more pertinently said by Bertie himself in his *Autobiography*. In any case, Bertie's feelings about Edith are clear from the moving poem with which he dedicated to her the *Autobiography* as a whole. Elizabeth and I still remember the day at Plas Penrhyn, just before the first volume came out, when Bertie showed us this dedication. From our point of view it was a heart-warming confirmation of the miraculousness of the change, from de-

pression and despair to happiness, which we had witnessed in
Bertie directly Edith came into his life. She had seemed to be—
and had turned out to be—everything that he could wish.

⟨✻✻✻✻⟩

Before Bertie went to Australia and the U.S.A. he had moved
to London, partly because Peter had sold the Ffestiniog house
and partly in order to provide a home in London for his elder
son John Amberley and daughter-in-law Susan, with their children. He had bought a largish house in Richmond and was installed himself on the second and top floors, with the Amberleys
on the ground floor.[1] This meant I could go and stay with him
for the meetings of A. J. Ayer's Metalogical Society. Bertie was
of course a member of the Society and we would usually dine
somewhere in the centre of London before going to the meeting.
I remember we did this in December of 1951. I have a characteristic letter from him asking me to 'stay on the 11th when you
read a paper' and adding: 'I don't think you need fear being
turned into a pug dog like the virtuous Swabian poet in Heine.'
After dinner, as we walked down Piccadilly towards Freddie
Ayer's flat in Whitehorse Street, Bertie was accosted by a charming and intelligent admirer whose obvious delight in having
actually spoken to his idol was set off for us by his also being
sufficiently in awe to apologize for invading Bertie's privacy.
(Most people take it for granted that if a person has been in their
house on the telly they need no further introduction. Even so,
being so new, the pleasures of conspicuous eminence were still
for Bertie greater than the pains.) As we walked on I remarked
on my own enjoyment of the reflection from his glory; and we

---

[1] Susan is the daughter of Vachel Lindsay, the American poet. One evening in
our house she gave a most rhythmically exciting recitation of several of Vachel
Lindsay's poems, including 'Congo'. This was remembered, she said, from her
father's own rendition. But the effect was very different from that of Richard
Hughes's recital on the B.B.C. Third Programme, recalled in 1968 from instruction also by Vachel Lindsay himself when Richard Hughes was at Oxford.
Richard Hughes's version was much more varied in pitch, with some parts almost
sung. But he said that it was in fact slower than Lindsay's own version: Hughes
simply could not make his voice go fast enough.

then talked about what I suppose could be called the sociology of awe, its function in a hierarchical society, and in particular about the sense of well-being which we tend to feel when deities or royalties 'condescend'. Bertie himself knew well from his childhood the sense of religious awe. And he also, he said, had found that he was in awe of Royalty. When he was given the O.M. by King George VI, he could not stop himself from being surprised— as are most people—at the royal condescension: how extraordinary, he felt, that the King behaves just like an ordinary human being!

The Metalogical Society had been started by Freddie Ayer in 1949 with the object of getting philosophers and scientists to meet and discuss problems which they felt had implications for, or relevance in, or perhaps even solutions in, each other's fields. Among the scientist members were J. Z. Young, the zoologist and anatomist, who delivered the 1950 Reith Lectures on *Doubt and Certainty in Science*, F. G. Young, the biochemist, Peter Medawar, also later a Reith Lecturer and Director of the Medical Research Council, Lionel Penrose, the geneticist, and G. J. Renier, the historian. The philosophers included Karl Popper, Stuart Hampshire, Richard Wollheim, J. H. Woodger, J. R. Thompson, Ernest Hutten, Robin Skynner (who was, however, a psychiatrist by profession), and Humphrey Slater (who had edited *Polemic*). Alfred Tarski, the logician, was one of the guests I remember. There were meetings once every month or so; and the society thrived for over four years, partly because Freddie Ayer kept the numbers down to a maximum of about fifteen at a meeting, so that discussion could be kept to a point. Bertie enjoyed the meetings very much, and so did I. However the society eventually faded out, I think—and so did Freddie Ayer—because of a failure of communication between philosophers and scientists. Part of the trouble was that the problems which worried the philosophers often left the scientists unmoved, and vice versa (but less so); part was that the scientists tended not to recognize as their own the aims and methods which the philosophers attributed to them.[1]

[1] And this was despite the fact that they certainly accepted Karl Popper's famous denial of the traditional theory that scientific method uses induction;

Russell's presence greatly enlivened the discussions at the Metalogical Society. Nevertheless he was not altogether in sympathy or in touch with the current linguistic trend in philosophical thinking. It was not merely that he did not appreciate what the linguistic philosophers were doing (despite the originally linguistic and analytical character of his own work); it was that he semi-deliberately misinterpreted their work, in order to be able to dismiss it, in the same sort of way as he misinterpreted Dewey in the example I gave in Chapter One.

⟨✶✶✶⟩

There follow some letters which belong in this chapter, and also three Journal entries which cannot be more precisely dated than to say that they also belong in this chapter.

---

i.e. the inference from observing that some As are B to the conclusion that all As are B. (Popper suggested that scientists use the 'hypothetico-deductive' method; i.e. the initial posing of a hypothesis, then deduction of the empirical consequences and finally observation to see if these consequences do in fact occur, in which case the hypothesis is confirmed—or at least not refuted.) What went wrong— in my opinion—was that the philosophers' conception of a scientific hypothesis or generalization remained different from that of the scientists themselves: the philosophers (including Popper) assumed that the task of science was to discover and establish what may be called 'absolute-all' statements. Thus a statement about the class of phenomena A (for instance, such a statement as 'Metals expand when heated' or 'Enzymes are proteins') was assumed to be legitimately asserted by a scientist as true only if it could be shown to be absolutely true (in all contexts— taken at its face value with no reservations) of all As past, present and future. Since it is clearly impracticable to show this (we cannot now observe all future As and in any case there are lots of exceptions to most scientific generalizations), the philosophers felt that the scientists ought to be more worried than they were about the philosophical problems of science. In practice the scientists find there is no problem; for, as 'empiricists' in the sense worked out on pages 56–7, they are normally content with statements which, when expanded and analysed, take the form 'As need to be treated as B for such and such a purpose'. (For example, 'Metals need to be treated, for the purpose among others of building houses, as likely to expand when heated.') Such a statement is more like a tendency-statement than a law; and it is not of course invalidated by 'exceptions' nor by our inability to observe all As. (In both these examples given here there are indeed exceptions: the new welded railway lines do not always expand when heated. When they are properly laid they are clamped down so firmly that they can't! Lysozome is now treated in some contexts as an enzyme but is not a protein.)

1948 or 1949

Most informative evening. Michael Burn came to drinks to
meet Bertie and to tell us about Hungary and Mindszenty.
Michael Burn gave the impression of being very objective—his
was the measured, anti-extreme attitude of the disillusioned.

[Michael Burn, author of *Yes Farewell*, had been till recently
The Times correspondent in Hungary. At the time of the
Hungarian Revolt in 1956 he was described by our local
paper as 'the well-known playwright and novelty'. He and
his beautiful wife Mary were also neighbours of the Russells,
and they became friends. It was Michael Burn, it may be
remembered, who wrote a most touching obituary note in
The Times, bringing out the pleasures—the warmth and
laughter and stimulus—of Bertie's company.]

Summer 1951

Drink party for Bertie. Rose Macaulay comes up from the
hotel; Hugheses, Blacketts, Jill and Tony. Tony knew Peter
(Russell) at Oxford. Rose Macaulay and Bertie compete in their
knowledge of the Bible. Bertie is probably the only living atheist
who knows so well what he is talking about.

[The Hugheses are Richard Hughes, author of *High Wind
in Jamaica,* and his wife Frances. Jill and Tony are my sister
and her husband, Anthony Greenwood. I remember there
was some discussion of the proliferation of atom-bombs
between Greenwood and Bertie. At any rate Greenwood
was eventually one of the group which included Russell
and which met in Canon Collins's house in January
1958 to launch CND. And in fact Greenwood was one
of the pioneers in the campaign against nuclear bombs even
before Russell.]

We were walking today on the harbour square in Portmadoc with Bertie and Peter. A man came up, and waited respectfully until Bertie turned to him.

'I do hope you will not think me impertinent in wanting to speak to you, sir', said the man. 'I have a great admiration for you.'

Bertie looked diffident and deprecating as befits the eminent author when approached by a fan.

'Very nice of you to say so.'

Peter looked pleased and proprietary.

'I enjoyed your book so very much,' the man went on. 'A marvellous evocation!'

'My *book*?' said Bertie with a query.

'Yes', said the man.[1]

Something seemed to be going wrong. Which or what could this evocation be, we wondered.

'Yes', the man repeated. 'Those wonderful sailing ships . . . what a fascinating sight this harbour must have been in those days!'

Collapse of everybody. The man had thought that Bertie was an—equally white-haired—Mr. Henry Hughes, who had indeed written one book, a very good one, called *Immortal Sails*, on the history of Portmadoc harbour.

CXVV₩Ω

Elizabeth and I have dozens of mostly shortish letters from Bertie, some of them merely planning his week-ends with us, or concerned only with such things as the doing up of the Ffestiniog house. However, some of the letters also contain characteristic and interesting passages. I think the best thing to do is to give an occasional letter complete, in order to set the form as it were, but otherwise simply to give extracts.

The first letter is in answer to Elizabeth's having written to say she had found a misprint in the American edition of the *History of Western Philosophy*. Elizabeth thinks she must have said that

---

[1] One of Bertie's favourite stories was of the doctor who, when asked by the proud father whether it was a boy or a girl, said 'Yes'.

she would eat her hat if there were not a misprint. But Bertie apparently misread:

> Trinity College,
> Cambridge.
> Feb. 20th, 1947.

My dear Elizabeth,

    You need not eat your heart out, as you are right about the misprint. I'm glad as the operation would be unpleasant, not to say dangerous. The misprint doesn't occur in the English edition . . .

> Penralltgoch,
> Llan Ffestiniog,
> Merioneth.
> 18.7.49.

Dear Rupert,

    I enclose cheque for whiskey. Do you remember Omar Khayyam: I often wonder what the vintners buy.

One half so precious as the stuff they sell. The question is relevant.

Thank Elizabeth for Yorkshire pudding etc.

> yrs ever
>
> William Collins.

[Whisky was rationed in those days.]

> 41 Queens Road,
> Richmond,
> Surrey.
> 4.5.50.

Dearest Elizabeth,

    . . . John and Susan have made the house very pleasant and comfortable. I hope you will both come.

> yrs ever
>
> BR

P.S. I have had my hair cut.

Usher's Hotel,
Sydney.
July 2nd, 1950.

Dear Rupert and Elizabeth,

I arrived here without misadventure, & so far have had quite a
pleasant time. I had heard of Australia as a land of drought, but I
arrived in a downpour, with floods everywhere and people in boats
rowing along railway lines. Now, however, the weather is delicious.
Though it is winter, roses are in bloom. Sydney & the harbour are
full of beauty, very like San Francisco. The people are like Americans,
except that they are less bumptious & don't hate England. I am saved
an immense amount of work by a charming young man appointed by
the Australian Foreign Office to look after me . . . . When there is
time he takes me to the Blue Mountains, which are delicious.

I should be enjoying myself but for worry about Korea. I have just
returned from dining with the Australian Foreign Secretary, Spender,
who does not think the Korean trouble will lead to a world war. I
think probably he is right, but I don't feel at all sure. I think the
Chinese *may* come in, & if so everybody will. I hate being so far from
home at such a time.

If there is likely to be war, I should like to have a refuge in North
Wales for John's family. . . . [Discussion about whether to buy a
house] . . . I fear I am asking a lot of you, but as soon as my work
is over & I get to bed, I am haunted by nightmares of atomic death,
& here, where I know no one, they drive me nearly mad. I wish I
resembled the Miller on the River Dee. Goodbye with more love

BR

Melbourne.
July 26th, 1950.

Dear Rupert,

. . . I think, even if the present war does not spread, Korea has made
a world war soon much more likely. The only hope I see is that

Americans may be frightened of their failure. But I don't expect that. So I strongly favour getting a house in Wales, & it should be got *now* before people are alarmed in England. Here people are much more conscious of Asia; they were alarmed when the Japs got into Papua, & have remained so.

. . . People here treat me well, except that I have been having a row with the Catholics because I said Asiatics ought to learn birth control. Catholics say they hope instead to teach them to live chastely in marriage!

There are two representatives of the King here, the Governor General & the U.K. High Commissioner (who counts as an Ambassador). Both are working men, both socialists, & both proud of it. One of them I knew in S. Wales in 1916, when he & I were on the verge of going to prison.

Love to you both. I am homesick & hate being so far away at this time. My views are utterly gloomy so I laugh all day.

yrs ever

BR

Menzies Hotel,
Melbourne.
2.8.50.

Dearest Elizabeth,

I enclose two pictures which need some explanation. A newspaper here said I looked like a 'sophisticated Koala'. I had never heard of a Koala. . . .

I have become very grand. I associate with Governors, Chancellors, High Commissioners & such. It will be a comedown when I get home. But I am desperately homesick. I hope it will be possible to buy Penralltgoch. Even if there is no war now, there will be one soon. . . .

Hotel Esplanade,
Perth. W.A.
11 August, 1950.

Dearest Elizabeth,

Enclosed may amuse you & Rupert. . . . Mannix is R.C. Archbishop of Melbourne. I have telegraphed to him demanding an apology. I have hopes of a good old row.

This is a pleasant smallish town on a broad estuary but the inhabitants are very Tory and Xtian. I long to be home. . . .

I am very gloomy about the world. It seems Korea will not lead to a world war, but there remain Formosa, Indo-China, Hongkong, Persia, Turkey, & Finland, not to mention Tito. I don't see how, with America in its present mood, we are to get through the next two years without a clash. . . .

[Archbishop Mannix had said: 'The United States refused Lord Russell admission, and I am sorry he was treated differently in Australia.' Unfortunately for Bertie's hopes, the Archbishop publicly admitted his error.]

41 Queens Road,
Richmond,
Surrey.
26.12.50.

Dearest Elizabeth,

. . . I had masses of work to clear away but am now entering upon a period of leisure which I hope will last the rest of my life. It will begin at midnight on Jan. 8th. That being so I could come to you on Jan. 9th. . . .

Sweden was great fun in retrospect. At the moment, much of it was boring. . . .

It is nice being treated like a Christmas tree!

Richmond.

2.1.51.

Dearest Elizabeth,

Alas I cannot come on the 12th. A lady, who may be described as a whirlwind, is descending upon me from New York. Her name is 'Public Interest Inc.' She was appointed by Columbia University to look after my publicity in New York, & she has since devoted herself to schemes (on a 10% basis, like St. Paul) for making me vast numbers of dollars . . . of which I shall be glad; in any case the lady is of the steam-roller type, & it is undesirable to stand in her way. She descends from the clouds on the morning of the 13th. I don't know how long she will stay, but she says she is going on to Paris and Rome to tell the French and Italian governments what to do, so I don't suppose she will stay long. As soon as I find out when she is going I will propose myself again. . . .

[This is the Miss Julie Medlock who is mentioned in the third volume of the *Autobiography* as having 'liberal and sympathetic views on international affairs'. She later came to stay with the Russells in North Wales, and they brought her to a grand house-warming party we had at Nant Pasgan to celebrate Elizabeth's at last having managed to buy the house. She very kindly gave the house the first copy we had seen of the

| PLAN AHEA |
| D |

notice.

Bertie was amused that his 'agent' should produce such an appropriate piece of linguistic self-reference. (His Theory of Types, with its hierarchy of languages, was designed to deal among others with paradoxes of the 'I am lying' type.) We have found, incidentally, that unless people have at least a touch of intellectual sophistication they fail to see the point of the notice; they are somehow unable to appreciate that a statement can be saying something which applies to itself.]

Richmond.

20.5.51.

Dear Rupert and Elizabeth,

May I come to you May 30—June 4 or part of that time? . . . I
meant to be idle at this time, but failed. . . .

I have finished a book of which my broadcasts are an abstract. I have
told America what I think of McArthur, & the Evening Standard what
I think of sex in America, & John what I think of sex in 41 Queen's
Road. This, with many broadcasts, has kept Satan out of a job. The
rest of the time I have enjoyed life. . . .

[The book was *New Hopes for a Changing World*, based upon lectures broadcast as 'Living in an Atomic Age'. Bertie had come a
long way from the pessimism of 1950. As he says in the *Autobiography*, this was largely because he had got through 'an immense amount of work and felt, in consequence, optimistic and
full of zest. [He] suspected that [he] had too much emphasized,
hitherto, the darker possibilities threatening mankind . . .'
(volume III, p. 31).]

Richmond.

20.7.52.

Dearest Elizabeth,

. . . I like your recipe of joining opposites. Do you remember
Tennyson's account of how Lancelot never got tired of Guinevere:

> His honour rooted in dishonour stood
> And faith unfaithful kept him falsely true.

Very profound.

I am sending Rupert a physicist's discussion of the question: 'Does
the question "does the neutrino really exist?" have any meaning?' I
think it is very good and quite what Rupert will like.

Much love, dear Elizabeth

yours ever

BR

[Elizabeth's recipe was for producing profound and purple writing; it consists of pairing off words whose meanings are contradictory—pride/humility, doubting/faith, etc. This will be found to give an instant purple tinge to statements, while the profundity is supplied by the fact that it can mean all things to all men.

The article was a draft of a lecture given by Sidney Dancoff, a brilliant young professor of theoretical physics at the University of Illinois, a few months before his untimely death in 1951. I think what Bertie liked in his thesis was the suggestion that the question was super-erogatory: the state of affairs in the field of molecular physics was such that Fermi was able to construct a theory which gave correct predictions and in which an important part was played by a set of symbols which Fermi named 'neutrino'. In this (precisely delimited) sense the neutrino 'existed'. To ask whether it existed in some more real way was pointless. Bertie was right in thinking I would broadly agree; though in fact I would have suggested that the question was indeterminate rather than pointless: whether we found it sensible to treat the neutrino (in our then current state of knowledge) as existing in the same sense as the electron existed would depend upon the context. Nowadays, of course, the answer is Yes in practically all contexts.]

> Richmond.
> 7.9.52.

Dearest Elizabeth,

Your letter about D. H. Lawrence was delightful to get—I am grateful to you for writing it. A lot of people have been angry with me about it. I have written a short story called 'The Guardians of Parnassus' in which all the villains are parsons. The worst of them is Professor of Pastoral Theology. I hope you will like it. I am filled with proud humility and submissive arrogance about it. . . .

[I think this must have been apropos of a broadcast which was later made the basis of the chapter on Lawrence in *Portraits from Memory*.]

20 Sep. 1952.

Dearest Elizabeth,

The news about your ear is very distressing. My heart goes out to you. What you say about your first rage & subsequent recovery of cheerfulness without bunk is very interesting and admirable. Edith (whom I hope you'll learn to call so) has a machine which is quite unobtrusive & very efficient, so that one seldom has to remember that she is deaf. I hope something of the sort will be possible for you.

I do not know when the October Metalogical will be. This is a secret locked within the breast of Professor A. J. Ayer. If he were to die tomorrow, there would be no way of ascertaining what date he had decided on, & therefore, on the verification principle, he would not have decided on a date, which is absurd.

A book of short stories by me is to be published some time next year. Two have villains who are parsons, but, *per contra*, two have charming bishops. I am now writing a longer one, which is to be savagely anti-religious—I am shocked about Robert Hughes.

Can I hope to see you when you come up in October? I should like to come to you when it suits—whether alone or with Edith I don't yet know. But it would be well to wait till we know about your ear, wouldn't it? Much love & very real admiration—

yours ever

BR

[Elizabeth had recently had a mastoid operation which had at first appeared to be successful in preserving her hearing but after all had failed. Bertie and Edith had come to see her in the London Clinic when she was hearing deceptively well; and we had had a party, gay with relief, embellished by moss roses from Edith and enlivened by a bottle of whisky from Bertie.

Elizabeth's deafness is relevant because Edith was already very deaf, while Bertie gradually became so, and because this affected our whole relationship by placing limits upon what could be said quickly and precisely in argument. As will be seen, this unfortunately meant that it became much more difficult—and sometimes impossible—to argue disputed points with Bertie. There is always a subtle process, in argument, whereby the degree of disagreement is verbally tempered to the claims of friendship. If this adjustment is to be effective, the words which operate it *must* be heard clearly at the first time of speaking. But these difficulties did not of course occur until much later—in the late 60s.

The letter is not headed, but was probably from Richmond. Bertie was most remarkably kind and sympathetic and considerate when unpleasant things happened to his friends. It is extraordinary to think that millions of people have believed that he was a cold, arid materialist.

Robert Hughes is Richard Hughes's elder son who had decided to go into the Church.]

Richmond.

October 30th, 1952.

Dearest Elizabeth,

Thank you for your letter. I have written to Ayer who closely resembles the Deity in his inscrutability. If and when he replies I will let you know. . . .

Bertie and Edith were married in December 1952; and from then on it was usually Edith who wrote to us. Here is an excerpt from a letter of hers of 8 June 1953, in which she tells the dramatic story of Bertie's very nearly dying seventeen years prematurely and being saved only by the 'new' antibiotics.

. . . It was an absolutely heavenly holiday & I'd much rather write you about it than about these following weeks. They've now pretty well eclipsed, for the moment, past pleasures, for they have been a series of miseries for Bertie, from the last of which he is only now beginning to convalesce. First he got a muscle torn in his back—horridly painful—then he had to undergo a series of X-rays & examinations of his insides, & then last Sunday the bombshell fell. We had a gay 'Sunday dinner' together (John and Susan are away holidaying) & after coffee I went up to my room to write letters, leaving him quite well

& happily embarking on a thriller. About an hour later he came up & said 'I'm afraid I'm ill'. And indeed he was, with bouts of rigidity & shudders & icy cold. I piled blankets & hot bottles on him & then tried to get help. We were all alone in the house. I tried every doctor whose name I knew on the 'phone—no reply. Then I tried our neighbours—no one at home. Everyone was on holiday that fine Sunday. In despair I rang the police. They sent a doctor—a savage man—fairly soon and got hold of our maid Dinah & in time sent our Richmond Dr. —who had sense & luck enough to call in a Harley Street specialist who lives in Richmond—& our London Dr. Boyd. The 1st police Dr. administered a drug which only made Bertie sick, & then he went off saying B. was all right & he himself must attend to his own patients. By the time the other three arrived Bertie was in agonies of pain and blue—indigo blue—in the face. They thought he could not live two hours. Thank God they were wrong. They diagnozed the thing right— as pneumonia—and the promptness with which they gave him one of these 'wonder drugs' & B's own vitality of course, pulled him through. Then they tried to get a nurse, even an assistant nurse— none to be had. Finally we were taken, about midnight, in the Richmond ambulance to the University College Hospital where, till yesterday, we've been ever since in a very pleasant private room. Bertie improved quite steadily & yesterday the Dr. drove us home again. Bertie seems like his old self, though he is naturally weak. . . . Bertie is asleep, or he would send his love of course. We often wish we cd. set off at once for N. Wales & see you & Rupert. *My* love to you too

                                                        Edith R.

Bertie himself then writes later in the month:

                                                        Richmond.
                                                        26 July, 1953.
Dearest Elizabeth,
    Thank you very much for your letter—you do write the most delightful letters. Your account of your Emily's visit made us laugh and laugh.

I had an illness about a month ago, but am now well. I couldn't quite make out what the Dr. said, but it seems there is a hole from my stomach to the lungs, & if I eat too much the food gets into the lungs, which don't like it. However I can't believe this is what the Dr. really meant.

I sent Rupert & you a story about the consolations of religion, which I hoped you would both like. But I had a letter from him from Luggala saying he had taken it away with him. I saw Luggala when I was 13, & it has remained an enchanted dream in my imagination ever since.

I seldom read anything serious, but I have lately read 2 books I liked: Deutscher's *Russia after Stalin* and Jowitt on Hiss, who, he thinks, may be innocent. . . .

[Emily had been our cook in London before the war. She remained in London throughout the war and afterwards. But she came every summer to us for her holiday, and we used to drive her about to see the sights. We took her to see Bertie at Ffestiniog some time in 1950, when he was there alone. Bertie behaved perfectly: he gave her a glass of sherry, asked her the conventional questions and smiled charmingly. Emily approved: she said afterwards to Elizabeth, 'I think he's a very nice friend for Mr. Rupert.'

Luggala is a white Regency Gothick house, set in its own valley and with its own lake, in the Wicklow Hills. It now belongs to Lady (Oonagh) Oranmore and Browne, but when Bertie saw it it must still have been part of the Powerscourt estate. Elizabeth and I found it as enchanting as did Bertie.]

CHAPTER FIVE

Elder Philosopher

In this chapter I propose to say just enough about Russell's relationship in the 1950s with current philosophy to explain his attitude towards the linguistic philosophers, and I hope also to explain some of the reasons for the somewhat unenthusiastic reception given to *Human Knowledge*, which caused him the disappointment described in Chapter Three.

The paper which Russell read to Ayer's Metalogical Society was entitled 'The Cult of "Common Usage" '.[1] At the outset Russell said that he did not want to misrepresent the 'linguistic doctrine' maintained by 'the most influential school of philosophy in Britain' at the time, which was 1952. Nevertheless he did, I think, misrepresent it. The doctrine ('as I understand it') he said, 'consists in maintaining that the language of daily life, with words used in their ordinary meanings, suffices for philosophy, which has no need of technical terms or of changes in the signification of common terms'. Russell then supported his objection to this alleged doctrine by pointing out—among other things—that the word 'mental' had in common usage the meaning 'mad'; and he observed that what the linguistic philosophers ought to have said they believed in was 'the usage of persons who have their amount of education, neither more nor less'.

There is some substance in the second part of this argument. It is true that the linguistic philosophers did not specify the meaning of 'common' or 'normal' usage precisely enough to prevent its being taken as 'vulgar' usage, nor to prevent argument among themselves as to what was in fact normal. All the same, it can be argued that Russell was mistaken in implying that the linguistic philosophers disapproved of technical words in talk *about* (as opposed to in) philosophical theories; and he also seems at least to some extent uncooperative in assuming that they *must*

[1] Reprinted in *Portraits from Memory* (1956).

have meant by 'common usage' vulgar usage. His argument was that they must accept the consequences of their failure to be precise. Nevertheless, the linguistic philosophers' interpretation was widely accepted; and the co-operative remedy would have been to ask for clarification rather than to assume the worst.

What the linguistic philosophers in fact claimed—or at any rate those whom Russell was attacking—was that the answers to many philosophical questions were given by treating common usage as correct usage. For instance, the answer to the question whether anybody can be said to know that some other person is in pain is given by finding out whether in common usage one would be able to say (correctly) 'I know that Freddie is really in pain; he is not just malingering'. By a natural extension of interest those philosophers who took this view of philosophical questions began also to notice that common usage was sometimes ambiguous or misleading. Then, by a further extension of interest, the philosophers started to analyse in detail the ways in which such ambiguous or misleading words function (the very existence of words like 'mind' and 'will', for example, misleads some people into thinking there must be entities which the words designate); and this stretches to cover also all the key-words of ratiocination, such as 'know', 'true', 'certain', etc. Then the real enthusiasts start analysing in greater and greater detail, making finer and finer distinctions of meaning—between different kinds of certainty about one's own future actions ('I am certain I shall refuse—because I always have refused in the past'—or alternatively 'because I just *am* certain'), between performing a speech action and performing a speech act, even between different kinds of speech act (some give a verdict—'assess'; some commit the speaker—'promise'; some exercise power—'appoint'; and so on).

Finally, with disagreement as to what precisely is the normal usage (and hence correct analysis) of a word or expression, there was opened up a whole new field of philosophical controversy. Can one correctly say 'I know I am in pain', or is this an unnatural locution? What precisely is the function of the word 'what' in 'I know what I am thinking'? Is it a synonym for 'that which' (i.e. a relative conjunction), or is it really an interrogative conjunction as J. L. Austin argued? Would it be sense to say 'I am not awake'? Or, to put this another way, does the statement 'I am not awake' entail its own negation? Is a mood like 'feeling sullen' strictly speaking *not* a feeling? Does the statement 'It looked like a duck to me' entail the statement 'I *noticed* that it looked like a duck'? What precisely does 'being responsible for something' entail? And so on.

These then were the kinds of question with which linguistic philosophy was concerned. Russell felt that they were trivial. And it is true that some of the philosophers themselves would probably have claimed no more than that they were intellectually diverting. On the other hand, there was a body of practitioners who took their subject seriously: they felt that the task of trying to answer such questions not only gave practice in reasoning but also clarified the workings of language and of the concepts which language helps us to manipulate. Whichever view be taken of linguistic philosophy—whether it be trivial or important in itself—it still failed in Russell's eyes to measure up to its responsibilities; that is, it refused to tackle the questions with which philosophy was traditionally concerned. And it was perhaps because, for him, these questions were both important and complex that he tended to regard linguistic philosophy as an intellectually lazy excuse for evading difficulties. And in turn it was because of this that he saw it as an activity which was concerned 'merely' with noting what was the common usage of various key-words and which in consequence denied the need for expertise by elevating common-sense above expert sense.

Apropos of this question Russell says in the third volume of the *Autobiography* (p. 37) that he received a letter when his paper on common usage was published 'from the arch offender saying that he approved, but that he could not think against whom it was directed as he knew of no such cult'. There do indeed seem to be few philosophers who would accept Russell's precise imputations. (It is significant that his paper does not contain any actual quotations from a practitioner of the cult.) There is a very relevant journal entry from 1956, which I will quote here rather than in its chronological place.

May 1956

Bertie, at drinks with Henry (Winch—the Explosion), very much on his form and telling his best stories.

After dinner here Bertie began discussing the problem (which has always puzzled him) of why his recent philosophical work has been so completely ignored by contemporary philosophers. We worked it out as being partly because philosophers are now giving up the 'logical' programme in philosophy; that is, they are beginning to accept that their theories cannot be logically proved—and hence they are giving up theories altogether. (This incidentally is why Urmson says that Russell's form of logical analysis does not work. Because there are no universally accepted 'rules of meaning' for ordinary language, no ordinary language proposition is ever strictly equivalent to any other.)

Bertie suddenly blew up and said that it was sheer laziness: 'These philosophers are simply too lazy to cope with the important problems; they know nothing; they know no Greek and no science; they are evading all the difficulties . . .', and so on.

Then, some minutes later, just at the end of the evening, he said:

'I suppose I am perhaps being unfair. It is very hard to reconcile oneself to the idea that one's chief work—and one's final conclusions—may be out of date.'

One reason why Russell objected to common usage as a criterion of correctness was, as I have suggested, that it elevated common-sense above expert sense as a criterion of truth. Thus, statements which give words their normal or common meanings tend (when correct) to express common-sense truths. It is common usage of the word 'know', for example, to say 'I know that Freddie has tooth-ache because he's told me so'; and it would be uncommon—eccentric and over-strict—usage to say, in the same circumstances, 'I do not know that Freddie has tooth-ache (because no empirical statements are certain).' Again, it is common usage of the word 'see', and common-sense, to say—when looking at the moon—'I see the moon.' Yet Russell claimed that this piece of common-sense was wrong. What we see, when looking at the moon, is—he said—a set of events going on inside our heads. To think we see the moon itself is naïve in the same way as it is 'naïve realism' to imagine that we can know there are real things in the external world.

The reason, in turn, why Russell objected to the elevation of common or naïve sense above expert sense was that, for him as a philosopher concerned to embody scientific knowledge in his scheme of things, the most important of the traditional questions of philosophy was the problem of knowledge; that is, the problem of justifying our claims to know things. It is the duty of the epistemologist (the philosopher concerned with the theory of knowledge) to query all such claims without fear or favour; and from Russell's point of view it was significant that the claims of common-sense have often been found mistaken in the history of expanding scientific knowledge. For this gave him an objective ground for pointing out the serious deficiencies of common-sense: if it could be so much at fault on some occasions, clearly it should not be made into an over-riding criterion of truth. However, there was also, I think, a subjective motive for Russell's attitude: the pleasure he always took in astonishing and discomfiting the common intellect could be indulged by showing that common-sense was often wrong in yet another field. Common-sense said at one time that the earth was flat and even now often says that the sun puts the fire out. Russell added to its discomfiture by insisting, as I have said, that it was quite wrong in imagining that when we looked towards the moon what we saw was an object in the sky rather than something going on in our own head and brain.[1]

I am inclined to think that this pleasure of Russell's in discomfiting common-sense, combined with the left-wing attitude of the temperamental sceptic (but these two tend in any case to

[1] I do not think there is any need here to assume that the one view contradicts the other. We can—less iconoclastically—say that the two views are complementary: the common-sense description of the situation is correct in everyday contexts, while the esoteric description may be correct from the point of view of the neurologist specializing in the mechanics of perception.

go together, since intuition disguised as common-sense is often opposed to expert sense), had a powerful influence on the direction taken by Russell's philosophical enquiries. Rather as a lawyer will be attracted by a surprising and even paradoxical judgement (a 'nice' point of law), so was Russell attracted by fields of enquiry where there was a good chance of showing that the truth was startlingly different from what everybody had taken for granted. He has even stated this somewhat élitist ambition in so many words. In the *Philosophy of Logical Atomism*, published in 1918, he said:

My desire and wish is that the things I start with should be so obvious that you wonder why I spend my time stating them. That is what I aim at, because the point of philosophy is to start with something so simple as not to seem worth stating, and to end with something so paradoxical that no one will ever believe it.[1]

I have already spoken of Russell's pleasure in pointing out that in *Principia Mathematica* the definition of the cardinal number 2 is reached (contrary to common-sense expectations) only after about 250 pages of prior definitions and deductions. I hope now to show that (again with the intent to confound common-sense) he was unkind to infinity. However, before doing this, I must follow up a reference I made in Chapter One to another sort of unkindness— Russell's semi-deliberate misinterpretation of the verification principle of the logical positivists. What this principle says in brief is that a proposition is meaningless unless it is verifiable. But this brief statement of the principle can of course be interpreted—expanded—in various ways, since the words 'meaningful' and 'verifiable' are seriously ambiguous. Interpreted conservatively and co-operatively, the principle says that a proposition is not factually significant (though it may be emotively meaningful, as with 'God is love', 'Stag hunting is wicked', for instance) unless one can specify a type of observation which would be relevant to confirming or disconfirming it. In this form the principle is widely acceptable; for it does not claim more than that meta-

[1] Originally published in the *Monist*. Reprinted in *Logic and Knowledge*, ed. by Robert C. Marsh (London, 1956), p. 193.

physical propositions like 'Everything is change' and 'Truth is beauty' have no factual significance. On the other hand, the principle can also be interpreted uncooperatively: the word 'meaning' can be assumed to cover all types of meaning; the word 'verify' can be taken as meaning only 'show to be true by direct observation'.

Russell's interpretation was, it seems to me, unco-operative in this way. He adduced the proposition 'It rained on Manhattan Island on the first day of the year I'. This proposition is of course meaningful not only in a quite ordinary sense but also in the specific (factually significant) sense with which the Principle of Verification is concerned. And, if we are co-operative enough to adopt the wider interpretation of the Principle, the proposition is also 'verifiable', since we can work out what sort of observations (such as seeing or feeling descending drops of water) would be relevant to deciding whether it is more probably true than false. Of course it is quite impossible to make these particular observations (Russell had been ingenious in his choice of example), but this is not the point. The point is that relevant physical observations are specifiable.

To a co-operative mind, then, the proposition is of the verifiable *type* and, as such, it is meaningful. But Russell was not concerned with this. He concentrated on the narrow interpretation, and thereby apparently showed that the Verification Principle can be reduced to absurdity. Because the proposition cannot be verified in the sense of being shown to be true by direct observation he argued that the logical positivist would have to deny the proposition any meaning at all. And he sometimes used the same argument to suggest that, according to logical positivism, all statements about what will happen in the distant future, when there are no more human beings, must also be meaningless.

❧

Now for Russell's treatment of infinity. His position was, I think, a direct consequence of his deciding to use the word 'similar' in a sense which, while being sufficiently like its ordinary sense to 'get by', was at the same time cleverly designed to confound common-sense by producing an apparently paradoxical situation.

It may be worthwhile trying to explain here how Russell played with, and amplified, this apparent paradox, since a similar process is I think at the root of most of the well-known paradoxes. The present paradox (which is the most familiar of the 'paradoxes of infinity') is engendered by pairing off in one-to-one correspondence on the one hand the infinite set of all integers and on the other hand the also infinite set of *even* integers:

1	2	3	4	5	6	7	.	.	.
2	4	6	8	10	12	14	.	.	.

The point about these two sets is that they can be paired off in this way indefinitely; there will always be one in the bottom row to pair off with one in the top row. So, in a sense, there are 'as many' in the lower set as in the upper set. The lower set, however, consists of every other term in the upper set. Therefore we would normally say that the lower set constitutes only a part, while the upper set is the whole, of the set of integers. So far there is nothing paradoxical. There is only a certain amount of vagueness in what we mean by saying that the lower set has 'as many' terms in it as the upper set.

It was one of the triumphs of the nineteenth-century mathematician Cantor that he worked out a precise way of categorizing this notion of 'as many' *in this context*. What he did was to extrapolate from everyday contexts to the esoteric context of infinity. In normal everyday usage we say that two flocks of sheep, for instance, are equal in (cardinal) number if all the sheep in one flock can be paired off in one-to-one correspondence, and without any remainder, with all the sheep in the other flock. Accordingly, Cantor stipulated that we should also say, when talking of infinite sets, that they have the same number of terms as each other when they can be paired off in this one-to-one relationship. And, henceforth, in the context of talk about infinity, the statement 'Set A has the same number of terms as set B' (or alternatively 'Set A is similar to set B'), was stipulated to mean 'The terms in set A can be paired off in one-to-one correspondence with the terms in set B.' Moreover—and this is the crux—it meant *only* this. It did not mean that the numbers of terms were equal in the everyday sense that the number of sheep in ten flocks of 30 each is the same as the number in five flocks of 60 each. In short, this definition of 'same number' and 'similar' was a special one, to be clearly differentiated from the everyday definition.

Now, provided we keep to this special definition of 'similar', there is no paradox in saying that the number of the infinite set of even integers is the same as the number of the infinite set of all integers, nor therefore is it paradoxical or surprising or in any way odd to say that the number of the part (the even integers) is similar in this special sense to the number of the whole (all integers). The reason why this is not odd or surprising or paradoxical is that, since special definitions are being used, it does *not* contradict the everyday axiom which says that in finite sets the whole is greater than any of its parts.

This special meaning of 'similar' has been useful in providing one way of defining an infinite set: an infinite set is one in which the number (in this special sense) of a part is similar (in this special sense) to the number of the whole. Because this definition has been useful in this way it has become widely current among mathematicians; but unfortunately it has come to be used rather carelessly, so that not only the lay public but some of the mathematicians themselves have assumed that it must have the same meaning in the infinity context as it has in everyday contexts. This is on the face of it understandable, since it has of course *somewhat* the same meaning, and since the whole process of reasoning with words is based upon our tending—in the absence of any indication to the contrary—to identify the meanings of identical words.

The result of this tendency to identify the meanings of 'similar' or 'equal' when used of infinite series with their meanings when used in everyday contexts is of course an apparent paradox. Here is a case where—at first sight—a familiar axiom of everyday life (that the whole is greater than any of its parts) seems to be contradicted. However, this appearance of contradiction subsists only

for the careless—or mischievous—eye. In fact, with a little tighten-
ing up of terminology the contradiction is not only shown to be
an illusion but does not even begin to gain substance. All we have
to do is to stress the distinction between the two uses of 'similar'
(or 'equal'); we could say, for instance, 'In infinite sets the part
is equal in a special sense to the whole', or 'A proper sub-set of
an infinite set is equivalent (in the sense that it matches one-to-one)
with the whole set'; or 'Whole and part of an infinite class have
the same number (in a special sense)'. But it does not of course
matter precisely how this distinction between infinite and everyday contexts is phrased. The prime requisite is that we should not
mislead anybody into thinking that the key-words are being
given their everyday meanings and hence into concluding that
the everyday axiom about parts and wholes is being denied.

And yet this is precisely what many of the mathematical theor-
ists (including Russell himself) have done. They have been unable
to resist the temptation to shock: not merely have they left out
the qualifying phrases about special usages; they have positively
encouraged people to believe that the everyday axiom about
parts and wholes has somehow been falsified. Eminent writers of
text-books, presidents of mathematical associations, etc., have
talked about the 'crude miracle' that a part of a set may be
equivalent to the whole, and about 'this contradiction to the
familiar truth'.[1] Russell's attack on the familiar axiom is even more
of a body-blow. 'The possibility', he says, 'that whole and part
may have the same number of terms is, it must be confessed,
shocking to common-sense.' And he delivers the knock-out by
refusing to help common-sense 'since I consider that, in the face
of proofs, it ought to commit suicide in despair'.

It is true that this is clearly a joke; it is also true that, a couple of
sections later in *Principles of Mathematics*, Russell does stress the
difference between the everyday and the special definitions of
'similar'. Nevertheless the joke is not innocuous. Damage has

---

[1] They are behaving like A. S. Eddington, the physicist, when he insisted that a
wooden plank is not solid in the ordinary sense, his sole ground being that all
substances are, in the physicists' context, masses of flying electrons with spaces
between them, and hence are not 'solid' in this very special sense.

been done in the very act of assuming that there is some sort of contradiction or oddity involved. It is this that makes me say that Russell (together with other eminent mathematicians) was unkind to infinity. The implication of this whole line of reasoning is that the surprises and shocks and oddities of infinite series have their source in the peculiarities of the infinite series themselves, whereas these surprises and shocks are, it seems to me, niggers in the ingenious woodpile of the human mind.

Having touched on mathematics I cannot leave completely unmentioned the work for which Russell is most widely celebrated. It can perhaps be epitomized—in slightly caricatured terms—by saying that, although Russell originally purported to show that mathematics was basically an elaboration of formal logic, what he finally agreed that he had done was to show that formal logic was unimportant except as embodied in mathematics. For there are in practice no situations where a decision is significantly aided by the symbolic calculus of formal logic: either the decision is so complex (as in working out benefits in a contributory pensions scheme) that a computer is needed (and a computer uses the simplest of logical manipulations—'and', 'or', 'not', etc.—at great speed; it does not use the convoluted deductive sequences of the text-books), or, if the decision is relatively simple, the symbolic calculus is redundant. Thus, Susan Stebbing, in writing her *Modern Introduction to Logic*, was herself unable to think of an example of what she called a 'simple' question which it was 'extremely difficult to answer . . . without the help of some form of calculus'.[1] She had to fall back on one which was invented by the logician Augustus de Morgan and which, she implies, anyone might plausibly wish to ask. This question is: 'What people are not the descendants of those who are not my ancestors?'[2]

~~~~~~

[1] *A Modern Introduction to Logic* (4th ed., London, 1945), p. 180.
[2] Even this problem is very easily solved without symbols by some people. For others I provide the answer. Divide people into two classes: descendants of my ancestors (D of A); and descendants of those who are not my ancestors (D of not-A). The required class is not (D of not-A). Therefore it is D of A.

Human Knowledge

I propose in this section, which concentrates on Russell's book *Human Knowledge*, to use some of the discussions which I had with Russell on its subject-matter in an attempt to describe for the layman what it was like to talk philosophy with someone who was a sort of paradigm of the traditional (as opposed to linguistic) philosopher.

(I must, however, acknowledge in advance that the point of view from which I approached—and now approach—philosophy is sceptical. As I have already said, I came gradually during these years to question many of the philosophers' assumptions, this necessarily including some of those accepted by Russell himself. I do not want to claim any undue weight for my views; but if I tried to suppress them it would distort the picture.)

For me the value of these discussions was greatly enhanced by the fact that I was not *in statu pupillari*. I could say boo to my teacher—I could pester him with questions about assertions and assumptions—in a way which would have been impossible if I had been a university student. I hope therefore that the reader will find this section informative at least about one aspect of what goes on in specialist philosophical circles. As will emerge, I think that many philosophers tend to play with meanings and to force them upon people in a peculiarly ingenious way. The point about Russell, in this context, was that he was a master of this kind of intellectual activity.

Russell, as a philosopher (rather than a pure logician), was primarily a sceptical epistemologist; that is, a man whose intellectual concern was to investigate the ways in which we attain knowledge and to search out, in order to eliminate, any false notions about how much we know. As he makes clear in his *Autobiography*, he had started out as a child with a passionate desire to find objective (and logical) certainty in our knowledge of the empirical world, but had been gradually forced to accept that this certainty was unattainable. Having thus been disappointed, he naturally wanted to make sure that no one else should be bamboozled by traditional ideas, as he had been, into assuming that knowledge was reliable when it was nothing of the sort.

In the grand tradition of philosophy Russell therefore set out to question the foundations of all knowledge—and in particular of the kinds of knowledge which common-sense naïvely left unquestioned (such as that what I see when I look at the moon is the moon). In 1946 he had already embarked upon *Human Knowledge: Its Scope and Limits*, which he intended to be, and has in fact turned out to be, his final summing up of the position as he saw it. Russell was greatly disappointed at the reception given to his book by the academic critics. I hope that what I say in this section will help to explain how this happened, and why he ought not to have minded as much as he did.

Having accepted that logical certainty was unattainable in empirical matters, and having also taken it for granted that the word 'knowledge' was strictly applicable only to propositions which were either completely indubitable or deducible from premises which were themselves completely indubitable, Russell had eventually come to the point of giving up the attempt to demonstrate that the foundations of empirical knowledge were secure. He decided instead to clarify the issue by first surveying the whole range of what we as human beings had been tempted in the past, and still wished, to call 'knowledge', and then carefully working out which parts of this purported knowledge could be said to be *justifiably* called knowledge.

Underlying the whole enquiry was a form of the Correspondence Theory of Truth—the theory which says that a true empirical statement is true in virtue of (and verified by reference to) its 'corresponding' in a fairly obvious sense with some fact in the empirical world which it 'describes'. 'The cat sits on the mat' is true if the designated objects and events are in the designated positions. (There is no need for present purposes to be more precise. This should serve to differentiate the theory from other theories of truth.) Empirical knowledge, then, was embodied in statements which were verified by our observing the empirical world and seeing—when they were true—*that* they were true. But what was involved in seeing that a cat sat on a mat? When someone claimed not merely that he had the *experience* called 'seeing the cat on the mat' but that there was indeed a cat sitting on the mat, how could he justify his claim?

Here was the crux of the problem. Russell was looking for some sort of *guarantee* that the claim was justified. If there was any possible doubt, then, he felt, it would not be strictly correct for us to say that we 'knew' there was a cat on the mat. And of course there was—there always is—a possible doubt in this very strict sense: we may conceivably be suffering from delusions. So, although the experience of seeming to see a cat on the mat may be indubitable, the inference from experience to purported reality is not. As Russell himself put it in talking about the question whether other people, with other minds, have the same experiences as us—and hence whether we can correctly say we know that other minds than our own exist:

Undoubtedly, it is through experiences of my own that I am led to believe in the minds of others; and, undoubtedly, as a matter of pure logic, it would be possible for me to have these experiences even if other minds did not exist.[1]

But even though Russell held this to be strictly true, he was by no means happy about it. He acknowledged that no one (not even himself and other sceptics) in practice doubts the existence of cats, mats, minds, etc. And it is of course precisely because we do not in practice doubt this 'common-sense' variety of scientific knowledge that the problem arises; if we did seriously doubt it, we should simply accept the situation. After all, it would not be surprising that such doubtful knowledge should have no firm foundation. Conversely (Russell argued) if we are right in placing reliance upon such knowledge—in not doubting it in practice—then the foundations must be secure; that is to say, there must be a set of principles and premises which can be shown to provide justification—if correct—for the inferences upon which we base this knowledge. His task, then, was to work out what were these justificatory principles and premises—what we would have to postulate to be true if we wished to validate scientific method.

[1] *My Philosophical Development* (London, 1959), p. 195.

But he went further: although he did not claim to demonstrate the truth of these postulates, he did suggest that there was at least some evidence in their favour. Thus, even though there were no ways of logically demonstrating the truth of such inferences as those which led us to believe in cats, mats, and minds, he could nevertheless collect numbers of instances where such 'non-demonstrative' inferences 'seem to us unquestionable' (op. cit. p. 194). And he took this unquestionableness as indicating that—in *some* sense at any rate—we are justified in treating our knowledge of the empirical world as valid. Accordingly, he took this validity as having evidential value in favour of the principles. 'The evidence in favour of the principles', he said, 'is derived from the instances [of non-demonstrative but unquestionable inferences] and not vice versa.'[1]

Russell is by no means alone in this habit of first assuming *that* we know certain propositions to be true, and only then enquiring *how* we know them. This assumption is at the basis of the whole controversy as to whether certain statements can be both synthetic (empirical) and at the same time *a priori* (i.e. known to be true without experience, as 'Two plus two equals four' is known to be true). One of these controversial statements is 'Nothing can be both red and green all over'. This is assumed to be known to be true quite independently of experience; it would, as they

[1] *Note for Philosophers.* Cf. the Preface to *Principia Mathematica*, second paragraph: '... the early deductions ... give reasons rather for believing the premises because true consequences follow from them, than for believing the consequences because they follow from the premises.'

Note for Empiricists (as opposed to 'philosophers'—cf. p. 56, note). Many people would I think deny that there is any need for the type of justification which Russell (together with epistemologists in general) was looking for. On Russell's own showing there is already *some* sort of justification; for, if he had no justification for saying that these inferences are unquestionable, then he should not have said it! (As he himself would have agreed, the fact that lots of people *believe* a proposition to be true is no evidence in its favour.) In fact, it seems likely that the reason why Russell accepted these inferences is the same as the reason why 'empiricists' do so. This is that, if we use them as on the whole reliable guides in dealing with the world and with our own experiences, we find that we are more often successful in making these experiences pleasant than we would otherwise be. In short, these inferences have a great practical value. This—for the empiricist—is in itself sufficient justification for treating them as valid; it would be superfluous to demand more.

say, be true in all possible worlds. Yet there seems to be no agreed way of formally demonstrating that it is true in this absolute sense. ('This is red' is formally contradicted not by 'This is green' but by 'This is not red'.) But there can be no justification for saying we know such a proposition to be true unless we can produce our grounds for saying it; so the controversy is the wrong way round. We cannot demonstrate that a proposition is true without first giving our grounds for saying it is true; and once we have given these grounds we have of course solved the problem of *how* it is true.

I raised this point with Russell in 1958, in connection with his saying on p. 82 of *An Inquiry into Meaning and Truth* (1940): 'We certainly know—though it is difficult to say how we know—that two different colours cannot cocxist at the same place in one visual field.' In our discussion he phrased his claim more colourfully: 'I see a fox over there', he said, 'and at a certain point on the fox's skin I see brown. Now I know that at that spot I do not see green—and indeed that I *cannot* see green. Yet I do not know how I know this.' I objected that it was not amenable to being known at all. For I could imagine the spot on the fox's skin to be just large enough for two colours to be visible on its surface. Russell then insisted that what he was talking about was a spot of a size such that it displayed only one colour. This, it seemed to me, was to argue in a circle. For unless this stipulated and restricted definition of 'spot' were made explicit and freely accepted in advance by the relevant company (in this case Russell and Elizabeth and I) the proposition remained potentially false and therefore *not* known. Alternatively, if the definition were explicitly adopted, then we would know how we knew the proposition: we would know that the reason why it was true was that it followed deductively from the (stipulated) definitions of the words contained in it. In short, the normal way round of our acquisition of knowledge is that we first work out *whether* we know something (this entailing our establishing *how* we know it if we do) and then—after all this—we may be justified in saying *that* we know it.

Unfortunately, Russell did not follow up this line of discussion;

he started to talk about incorrigible statements (i.e. statements like 'I feel hot'— as opposed to 'I am hot'—which no one else can have any ground for denying or confirming and which are therefore in a sense 'uncorrectable'). These were relevant in the context because there is a sense in which we just *do* know such statements, and the question how we know them is inapplicable.

I have gone into this point in some detail because it seems to me to throw an interesting side-light on the mental processes of philosophers who belong to an intellectual élite. Although Russell held many anti-establishment views, this was in his case due much more than usual in a reformer to the clarity of his thinking: he usually rebelled rather because he saw that the *status quo* was indefensible than simply because he felt rebellious. He was not therefore the type of reformer (like D. H. Lawrence and some educationalists) who are right for the wrong reasons—because the *status quo* is so horrible that anything different could not help being an improvement. This means that he was able to be anti-establishment and anti-élite while at the same time remaining a member of the élite to his intellectual (and emotional) marrow—as in his fireworks over the building of the Ffestiniog house.

One of the characteristics of élitist thinking in the past was a readiness to believe that certain things could be known by authority of authority—whether this authority be God or the priests or the current ruling class. If it were obvious to all the members of an élite that some proposition were true, then this in itself was psychologically a sufficient guarantee of its truth. These 'socially guaranteed' propositions were what constituted the corpus of *a priori* knowledge; that is, of purportedly eternal and universal truths about the constitution of the universe, about being, about right and wrong, etc., which were held to be known independently of experience, so that there was no need to look at the empirical world to see whether they were true. And this corpus of establishment belief (establishment, because it is in effect the authority of the establishment which decides which of a number of equally untestable and therefore equally unjustifiable beliefs shall in fact be 'established') was large, secure, and influential until well into the present century. So Russell may well have been somewhat predisposed by his intellectual environment towards the kind of thinking which assumed there was an informative potential in *a priori* statements.[1] In any case his philosophical thinking at Cambridge and for some years after was firmly based in the idealist position—the position which holds that the external world is of so little importance and reality in comparison with the world of ideas that in extreme cases it does not even exist. (He admired Bradley more than any other recent philosopher!)

Certainly, when I started learning philosophy from Russell and others I noticed that there was a curious mixture of tentativeness and confidence in the way in which philosophical views were stated: philosophical *theories* would be put forward in a tone which allowed that alternative views, though wrong, might nevertheless have points in their favour and would be listened to in a gentlemanly manner. The initial *premises* though (that is, the assumptions about proper usage and rules of reasoning which underlay the whole discussion) were in a very different case: they would be put forward (if at all—many of them would of course remain unstated) in a tone of emphasis which took them completely for granted—so much so that any attempt to question them would be met at first with unconcealed astonishment and then quite often with the assertion or re-assertion in a loud and confident voice of the proposition in question.

When Russell was relying upon such taken-for-granted premises the confidence in his voice was supreme. I well remember the first time Elizabeth and I discussed the problem of knowledge with him. We were both still philosophically naïve: we imagined that there were all sorts of empirical propositions which we could know with certainty to be true—such as that the sun will rise tomorrow, that it is raining now if we can see and feel the rain, that a man run over by a steam roller will die . . . etc. But our

[1] The general view now (though somewhat complicated by the controversy about statements like 'Nothing is both red and green all over') is that the only *a priori* truths are mathematical and/or logical ('Two and two make four', for example) and that they are not informative but are purely verbal in the sense that they are merely deductive consequences of the definitions of the words contained in them.

everyday confidence in our common-sense certainties was no match for the esoteric confidence of Russell's scepticism. When he found that we were not completely deflated or convinced by flat statements like 'It is not certain that the sun will rise tomorrow', he stepped up the pressure. He asked us what *possible* reason we could have for expecting the sun to rise tomorrow; and when we talked about its always having risen in the past, he banged the arm of his chair and said: 'But you have *no* grounds whatsoever for thinking that what has happened in the past will continue to happen in the future.' (This of course is the genesis of the Problem of Induction.)

Eventually this kind of pressure prevailed. There were two factors involved, which reinforced each other. In the first place, there was the tone of authority in Russell's voice, which was implicitly so confident that one felt there simply must be something in what he was saying, even though he himself did not in fact produce any grounds whatsoever for his assertions. In the second place, this impulse to accept what Russell said on his own say-so was reinforced by a tendency which is I think present in all reasonably social human beings, since communication would be impracticable without it. The point is that words in general are ambiguous (and none the worse for that of course). Any given sentence, therefore, may—and often does—have a number of possible interpretations, only one of which will have been intended by the person uttering the sentence. In many cases the intended interpretation will be indicated by the (physical or intellectual) context. Thus, the interpretation we give to 'This grass is not smooth' will be different if we are standing on a bowling green from what it will be if we are standing on a football field; again, the interpretations we give to the words 'logical' and 'philosophical' will be very different in logical and philosophical contexts from what they will be in everyday contexts. However, such environmental indication of the context will often be insufficient to give a definite clue. In such cases the speaker should ideally state his meaning explicitly. But this of course is very seldom done in practice since it would make communication intolerably prolix. What usually happens is that the

audience picks up—more or less accurately—the speaker's meaning from various clues, including (and this is the point) the
inferences which he implicitly draws from the taken-for-granted
definitions.

Clearly, this process of picking up the clues is quite essential for
communication. What I am suggesting therefore is that as social
animals we are born with a powerful impulse to co-operate in
this way when talking: we go on trying out more or less un-
consciously the various possible meanings of the words involved,
rejecting those meanings which do not 'fit' (i.e. which do not
allow the conclusions which the speaker is drawing) and finally
hitting upon the meanings which do fit—which make sense of
what the speaker is saying. Since we are in a co-operative mood
we naturally adopt these meanings as the correct ones in this
context. What is more, if we have the slightest tendency towards
belief in Proper Meanings (as do most people with an interest in
literature and language) we find ourselves tempted to think of
these meanings not only as appropriate in this context but as the
only correct ones absolutely.

This is what happened to Elizabeth and me over the philosophers' meaning of the word 'know'. When Russell insisted with
such authority that, despite our past experience, there was no
justification for saying we 'knew' the sun would rise tomorrow,
we found of course that the only way in which we could make
sense of what he was saying was to reject all the everyday meanings of the word 'know' and to restrict it drastically to that usage
which insists that we cannot correctly say we know something
unless we know it with indubitable certainty. Directly our sub-
conscious verbal apparatus had grasped that this must be the
meaning which Russell was giving to the word, we did of course
give the word this meaning ourselves. And there would have been
no harm in this co-operative attitude if we had confined it to the
current discussion. But Russell's argument—and indeed most of
the philosophical arguments about knowledge—depended upon
the meaning being accepted not merely in the restricted context
of philosophy but universally—as the One True Meaning. We
had to accept this as well.

It was here that Russell's air of authority operated most effectively. If he had stated explicitly that he was restricting the meaning of 'know' and if he had asked us to accept this restriction as applying universally, we would almost certainly have jibbed. As it was, our desire to co-operate reinforced his air of authority, and we found ourselves accepting the meaning unawares, as one accepts the card forced upon one by a conjurer.[1]

There was I think a further factor impelling us to accept Russell's implied definitions—a factor which has a strong influence on much philosophical reasoning. I have already suggested that there is a tendency in people who have a 'feeling for words' to believe that words have True Meanings. It seems to me likely that this tendency affects the sub-conscious reasoning even of those who with their conscious reason completely reject the notion of True Meaning. This certainly used to happen with me, and I think it happened also with Russell. For, although he firmly and

---

[1] This may suggest that some of the problems of knowledge are products of arbitrarily restrictive definitions. I think that this is probably so (and that the same applies to many other philosophical problems). The problem about knowing that the sun will rise tomorrow is typical of many problems which are embodied in questions of the form 'How can we know that such and such is true?' Here the underlying assumption is that something is wrong. We seem not to know, and yet we feel we *ought* to know: on the one hand we find—given our strict definition of 'know'—that we cannot know, for example, that the external world exists, while on the other hand we feel we do know this in *some* sense. If we were to acknowledge that we are here using the word 'know' in two senses the problem would disappear: we would simply say that the proposition 'The external world exists' is not known with indubitable certainty but *is* known with the practical certainty which is adequate for everyday purposes. The problem only arises if we fail to make up our minds whether we are going to count this latter (everyday) usage as legitimate. If we decide that it *is* legitimate, then we must acknowledge that there are two meanings of 'know' involved; and no problem arises. If, on the other hand, we decide that the everyday usage is not legitimate, then we must acknowledge that we just don't know that the external world exists; and again no problem arises. What in practice happens—at least with some philosophers— is that although they intend to reject the everyday meaning (since it is loose and imprecise), they cannot eradicate their normal tendency to rely in everyday situations upon everyday certainties, and consequently they find that they are automatically treating the everyday usage as legitimate enough at least to create a puzzle. In short, although they assume that they are using the word 'know' in a single strict sense, they are in fact shifting between the two senses. How can we know (sense 1), they complain, when we do not know (sense 2)?

explicitly denied True Meanings, he often talked in a way which implicitly invoked them. Thus, the very fact that he did not at once qualify his use of the word 'know' (i.e. indicate what *kind* of knowing this involved) suggests that he had not thought of himself as having selected one meaning from several legitimate variants, and this in its turn suggests that he did regard the word as having one 'proper' meaning which we could not but recognize, our puzzlement being therefore a matter merely of our taking rather a long time to see the simple logic of what he was asserting.

A similar situation arose some years later when Russell and Ayer were expounding to Elizabeth and me a philosophical puzzle called the Paradox of Confirmation. This was apropos of a paper by David Pears, then a young and relatively unknown philosopher, on 'hypotheticals', which we had been reading and discussing, I remember, partly because it was beautifully written in a subtly esoteric style. We were like painters admiring a painting for its technique as much as for its content. In the course of his paper Pears offered an explanation of the Confirmation Paradox. A key component of this paradox, for reasons too complicated to explain here, is a general statement of the form 'All ravens are black', sometimes expressed in the hypothetical form 'If anything is a raven it is black'. And one of the questions raised is whether the observation of a black raven verifies and/or confirms this statement.

In my opinion the question depended to some extent upon how the sentence 'All ravens are black' is intended to be interpreted. A logician would of course intend it to be taken strictly as meaning that all ravens whatsoever are black, and hence as not verified until we have in fact examined all the ravens in the universe (past, present, and future). On the other hand, an ordinary bird-lover instructing a class of children might well intend it in the same spirit as he would a statement like 'All wasps have stings, but not all bees'. In the first case, the observation of a single black raven does not verify or even confirm the generalization; the only observation of a single raven which *would* do so would be that of the last raven in the universe, all the others having been already observed. In the second case—the everyday—what is involved is in effect a 'rule of expectation': 'Act on the assumption that any ravens you meet will be black.' Here the observation of a single black raven would certainly be counted as a confirmation of the value of the rule. And, what is more pertinent to the paradox, the observation of (say) a couple of albino ravens would not falsify the rule, though it would of course falsify the logicians' strict generalization.

As can be seen, one can easily manufacture contradictions if one assumes that the statement 'All ravens are black' has One Proper Usage, or (to put it more precisely, in philosophers' terms) if one assumes that the sentence 'All ravens are black' can express only one statement, while in fact—as in the case of the two kinds of knowing—one is sub-consciously treating it as embodying two distinct statements. This is I think the key to the paradox; for what confirms one statement does not confirm the other. However, at the time I was only feeling my way towards the idea that there was something potentially ambiguous somewhere. So I asked for guidance; I asked what exactly was meant by 'All ravens are black'. And I got very much the same reaction as with the word 'know'. 'It means', said Russell, 'precisely what it says. "All ravens are black" means "*All — ravens — are — black*".' And Ayer backed him up.

If I am right in thinking that there was a touch of élitist authoritarianism in Russell's attitude towards some of the basic premises of philosophy, then it may throw light on the kind of prestige which has always attached to philosophers and to philosophy in establishment circles. But this is merely a beguiling speculation. In Russell's case the point I am making is only that this authoritarian confidence may have encouraged him to believe that he could know something to be true without knowing how he knew it; that is, without knowing what criterion of truth he was using—and indeed while implicitly assuming that his and his group's confidence in a proposition was in itself a confirmation of its truth. It was an indirect result of this confidence that he saw his accomplishment in the enquiry into human knowledge as important not merely in working out what principles would be needed *if* scientific method were valid, but also in providing evidence that these principles were in fact probably true. And it was I think partly because Russell felt *Human Knowledge* to be important in this way that he was so disappointed by its reception. It was intended to be a definitive statement of how little we could know with certainty about the empirical world and also of what we could nevertheless count as very probably true.

But *Human Knowledge* was published at a time when the dominant school of philosophy in Britain and the U.S.A. had largely abandoned the task of answering traditional philosophical questions (partly I think because it was becoming too obvious that there was something wrong with the methodology of a discipline which had not answered any of its questions definitively in two thousand years). Instead of traditional enquiries into the nature of truth, beauty, goodness, obligation, power, etc., the philosophers were turning to enquiries into the nature of the language in which the traditional enquiries had been made, one hypothesis being that the unsolved problems and general inconclusiveness of traditional philosophy were products of our failure to understand how language works. This investigative and 'problem-solving' attitude towards language ran parallel, as I have already explained, with the more purely descriptive work of people like J. L. Austin and also with the work of the 'ordinary language' school, which claimed that there were no problems of knowledge, since it was perfectly correct (because accepted as normal) usage to say that we knew all sorts of things about the external world.[1]

The result was that, although *Human Knowledge* was reviewed in the main respectfully, it was not taken as the definitive work which Russell felt it to be. It goes without saying that he would

---

[1] The relationship between all these approaches is so confused that no single account would be accepted by the generality of philosophers. There is even disagreement as to what G. E. Moore was *really* defending in his famous 'Defence of Common Sense', which helped to initiate linguistic philosophy, and in which he flatly says, as against the solipsists, that he *knows for certain* that there are other living beings. Despite it being commonly assumed that Moore was talking about language—claiming that ordinary linguistic usage is correct usage—some people say that his title was in fact apt: he was simply arguing that common-sense beliefs are correct beliefs.

not have objected to its being seriously criticized. What he minded was that its objects and aspirations were not accepted as warranting serious study. And one of the factors which—in his eyes—was indeed a warrant of its importance was that the whole enquiry was scientific: it assumed that the scientific account of the world was to be preferred to any other, and it also took seriously the question whether the foundations of scientific method were secure (in the same way that Russell's task in *Principia Mathematica* had been to enquire whether the foundations of mathematics were secure). It is perhaps worth stressing here that Russell's valuation of scientific method was high because he considered that it provided the only method of gaining objectively testable knowledge. He was always very firm with those who argue that some other method of enquiry could provide equally valuable knowledge, and who base their argument upon the (perfectly correct) premise that scientific method does not produce objectively testable judgements in the field of aesthetics and (pure) ethics, combined with the (quite erroneous) premise that there must be *some* method which does do so. He puts the case very concisely in *Religion and Science*:

While it is true that science cannot decide questions of value, that is because they cannot be intellectually decided at all, and lie outside the realm of truth and falsehood. Whatever knowledge is attainable must be attained by scientific method; and what science cannot discover, mankind cannot know.[1]

Unfortunately the fact that the foundations of scientific method were at stake had no bearing upon how *Human Knowledge* itself was evaluated. The direction which current philosophy was taking was—as always—largely conditioned by intellectual fashion; and at that time linguistic philosophy was in fashion, while worries about knowledge and the problem of induction were out. This is why I feel that Russell ought not to have minded so much as he did the neglect of his clarifying thesis: it was not

[1] 1935, p. 243. (It is a significant fact that one can indirectly define 'scientific evidence' by noting that, although it will often be rejected as evidence *against* a cherished belief, it is the only kind of evidence which all people, of whatever creed or temperament, will always accept in *favour* of their cherished beliefs.)

thought to be wrong or beneath notice; it was simply out of fashion. On the other hand it *was* a definitive work; and Russell very naturally found it galling that no one should notice this. It seems to me that (given the currently accepted philosophical assumptions about Theory of Knowledge) Russell made a water-tight case for saying to philosophers: 'Either you become a solipsist of the moment, or you acknowledge that the validity of scientific method depends upon acceptance of my five postulates— or you stop theorizing about knowledge at all.'[1]

Russell was as firm about solipsism of the moment as he was about the scope of scientific method. He made it quite clear in *Human Knowledge* that ordinary solipsism is a pusillanimous half-measure; the solipsist has no right to try and exempt himself from the (past and future) non-existence which he imposes upon everybody else. What is more, as Russell acknowledged, he himself had no water-tight way of refuting solipsism of the moment. But he felt that he was justified to some extent in relying upon 'robust common-sense'. As he said (on p. 515): 'If . . . anyone chooses to maintain solipsism of the moment, I shall admit that he cannot be refuted, but shall be profoundly sceptical of his sincerity.'

However, although the case for the five postulates as an alternative to idiotic solipsism may be completely made out, it is arguable whether Russell was right in claiming further that a positive probability attaches to the postulates. But this is beside the present point. The fact remains that Russell produced a large and comprehensive work on the subject which was nearest to his intellectual heart, and that it produced little response from the philosophers to whom it was addressed.

---

[1] Ordinary solipsism is of course the doctrine that the solipsist himself is the only self that can be known to exist, all other apparent selves being figments of his mind. Solipsism of the moment holds that the solipsist can know only that he himself is at the moment existing and experiencing; there is no justification for inferring even that he existed a moment ago or will exist in the future.

CHAPTER SIX

Strong Feelings

IN 1953 John and Susan Amberley left the Richmond house, and John himself fell seriously ill. The Russells were left to cope on their own with John and Susan's three very young children. It seemed that one way of coping would be to take a house somewhere in the country which was large enough to hold all of them, plus a nanny; and to have a small house or flat in London as well.

Elizabeth and I began to look for houses round about Portmeirion. And for the next two years we inspected various possibilities, with Bertie and Edith occasionally coming up to look at anything that seemed reasonable. Luckily—despite there not being unlimited time—we rejected them all on one ground or another. For in 1955 there became available Plas Penrhyn, which was almost ideal. It was a medium-sized Regency house, with its own grove of beech trees, which belonged to a neighbour and friend. It was on the Portmeirion peninsula (though not actually on the Portmeirion Estate), and—best of all for us—was only five minutes' walk away. It had been built (partly out of two already existing cottages) by the same architect as had built the house across the Portmadoc estuary which belonged to Shelley's friend Madocks. (See the *Autobiography*, vol. III, pp. 71-2.) And it had one unusual feature in common with the Madocks house: in several of the rooms there was a window directly above the fireplace. The actual advantages of this arrangement were not great; indeed it meant that you had the light in your eyes when reading before the fire. But it intrigued people, who did not at first see what was odd and then were puzzled as to how the smoke got out. (In case the reader is also puzzled I should explain that the flue started off sideways and then went up beside the window, with a trap-door for cleaning in the outside wall.) The drawing-room fireplace and window turned out, as it happened, to be a positive asset. There was a small conservatory on the outside wall of the drawing-room, which Bertie and Edith filled with masses of flowers set up on shelves so that there was always a jungle of colour to be seen over the fireplace. From the other window, which was a half French window with steps up and down to the verandah, there was a marvellous view of Snowdon to the north and of the sea and estuary to the west. Bertie was delighted with the house, and the view, and the beech trees. It was all very satisfactory.

However, this was still two years ahead. In the interval Bertie's life was as busy as usual. With Edith to help organize his correspondence, he got down to articles, Brains Trusts, broadcasts, and the writing of books (most of *Human Society in Ethics and Politics*) and short stories. The only thing that interrupted his life at this moment was a prostate operation in January 1954, from which — as usual—his recovery was amazingly quick, even though there was one set-back. In a letter to Elizabeth dated 9 February, Edith wrote:

. . . Bertie developed a slight fever on Sunday, and, of course must stay in hospital. . . . I am very anxious as the doctors, though they have made every test they can think of, cannot find the cause. . . . Penicillin they tried, & it was no help. So now they are trying other drugs . . .

One of the drugs they tried was M & B. These were the early days of such drugs, and M & B still tended to depress people. Bertie was very much affected by it; and afterwards he told us how curious it was to have this absolutely inescapable feeling of misery and gloom while knowing perfectly well that there were no grounds for it. It gave him an extra insight into how easy it is to believe things simply because one feels them strongly.

One of the pleasures of marriage for Bertie and Edith was that they were able to go away for leisurely holidays together. In these years they went to Scotland, Paris, and Greece. In April and May 1954, when Bertie had completely recovered from his operation, they went to Scotland and then stayed with us for a week on the way home.

13 May 1954

Took Bertie and Edith over to Plas Newydd for lunch. Great success. Bertie in fine form. The Whistler room overwhelmed them, as it does everybody. Bertie and Henry exchanged gossip about the enterprising behaviour of their respective ancestors in the time of Henry VIII.

[Plas Newydd is the Marquess of Anglesey's house on the Menai Straits. The Whistler room is a narrow forty-foot-long dining-room, almost entirely covered with wonderful *trompe-l'œil* painting by Rex Whistler, and with windows only on one side, so that the deception is miraculous.]

Here is Bertie's bread-and-butter letter:

Richmond.

21 May, 1954.

Dearest Elizabeth,

We have been meaning to write & say what a perfectly delightful time we had staying with you, ever since we got home. But first there were letters—Turks, Finns, Japs, etc. not to mention a few from people I knew. Then there was my birthday, which kept Edith very busy, as we gave a party. (I wish you and Rupert had been at it.) We were honoured by a gate-crasher who said he was a friend of Freddie Ayer, but Freddie didn't know him from Adam. The rest of our guests wondered why we had asked him, as he didn't seem very bright. We didn't know he was not Freddie's friend until he had gone. Then we counted the spoons, but as none were missing his motives remain mysterious.

Your forget-me-nots were lovely and your food delicious. In the few intervals between sensual pleasures the conversation was good enough to make one forget the next meal. Seriously, it was very delightful seeing you both. Edith, who may be deemed to have written this letter, but is worn out with typing for me, sends her love.

Yours ever

BR

(In a later letter Edith said the gate-crasher had an orange moust-ache. I wonder if anyone can identify him.)

⦜⦜⦜

Bertie was as good at writing bread-and-butter letters as he was at every other kind of writing. It seems likely that one element in his influence as a thinker was simply that because he was so fluent he wrote an enormous amount. During the last fifty or so years anyone wishing to enquire into some problem of human behaviour would almost certainly have been advised (by the liberal minded) to read one of Russell's books; for there would be sure to be one at least which dealt with the problem in question. But of course it was not only the great scope and volume of Russell's writings which enhanced his influence. What he said was always patently *sensible*: it was clear, concise, logical, and humane. However extreme Russell may have been in his feelings about his currently favourite campaign, it must not be forgotten that he was in most fields extraordinarily wise, in the sense that he knew which elements in his enormous range of knowledge were appropriate—and in what weights—to any particular case. (This, it seems to me, is decisively confirmed by the collection of letters to the public which appears in *Dear Bertrand Russell*.)[1]

One of the activities which occupied him in 1952–4 was the writing of the partly satirical short stories published in *Satan in the Suburbs* and *Nightmares of Eminent Persons*. These were as beautifully written as ever, but in a formal eighteenth-century style which was out of fashion, and with an intellectual tenor which was also I suppose out of fashion; the sentiment, especially in the *Nightmares*, was urbanely anti-clerical and satirical, with under-stated jokes. I found I enjoyed these stories very much. But they did not get good reviews, except—notably—from Angus Wilson in *The Observer*. Bertie was rather sad that Stanley Unwin refused to publish these stories; but Allen & Unwin do not of course normally publish fiction. In a letter answering one of mine, about

[1] Ed. Barry Feinberg and Ronald Kasrils (London, 1969).

the story called 'Faith and Mountains', Bertie said he had trouble even with John Lane, who did publish the stories. Their reader was apparently upset by Bertie's assumption, in a pastiche of what he called the Tempora Supplementary Letters, that the *T.L.S.* would extol intuition and Eternal Verities as against 'mere observation of brute facts'. 'John Lane's reader', he says, 'wanted me to cut out the bits you like from the *T.L.S.* & the passage about heresies beginning with M, but I refused.'[1]

⟊⟊⟊⟊

During all this time Bertie was gradually consolidating his attitude towards the H-bomb, this culminating in the foundation of the Pugwash Conferences in 1957 and in the formation of CND in January 1958. I do not propose to attempt a detailed description of the controversies which ensued. The whole thing has been already fully documented in the *Autobiography* and in the files of the newspapers. In any case it is not my object here to write a biography or part of a biography. I am hoping only to fill out a portrait. Accordingly, I shall say only enough about Bertie's various controversies to set the scene for the characteristic incidents which I quote from my journal.

One typically exciting moment with Bertie has to be seen in the light of his being passionately opposed to Britain's having the H-bomb, whereas the Labour Party's policy was the opposite. It so happened that Elizabeth and I had many discussions during that time (1957 onwards) not only with Bertie but also with John Strachey (who was incidentally Amabel Williams-Ellis's brother). As a front-bencher Strachey agreed broadly with the Labour Party's policy, and he had accordingly written articles and pamphlets putting forward the case for our having the H-bomb. Bertie's argument was based in part upon the assumption that Britain would be the first country to be wiped out—unless it was ostentatiously unarmed—in an atomic war. John Strachey, on the other hand, took the 'balance of terror' view: he felt that the best way to prevent a war altogether was for us to co-operate in NATO policy.

[1] *Nightmares of Eminent Persons* (London, 1954), pp. 133 and 143.

Elizabeth and I found ourselves completely undecided on the question of expediency. There were so many arguments on both sides, and so many unmeasurable factors involved, that we gave up trying to decide the issue at this level, and fell back on the maxim: When in doubt, do not plan to kill a lot of people. This meant that, although we did in fact agree with Bertie's conclusion, our grounds for doing so were very different from his.[1] And it also meant that we were sufficiently sympathetic to John Strachey's view to be able to appreciate it and retail it to Bertie.

The week before the journal entry which follows, Elizabeth and I had stayed for a few days with John and Celia Strachey at their house in Essex.

24 July 1958

Bertie and Edith came for drinks.

When we said we had been to John and Celia's and had discussed the H-bomb, Bertie asked me what line John had taken. Although I tried to make it clear that I was simply describing John's argument rather than advocating it, Bertie was so angered by it that he simply couldn't divorce the message from the messenger: he took it for granted that I must be on John's side. (He was particularly annoyed by John's saying that if necessary Britain could withdraw from an American venture.)

'You and John Strachey—you belong to the murderers' club,' he said, banging the arm of his chair. The murderers' club, he explained, consisted of people who did not really care what happened to the mass of the populace, since they as rulers felt that somehow they would survive in, and because of, privilege. 'They make sure of their own safety', said Bertie, 'by building private bomb-proof shelters. . .'

I brought Elizabeth and Edith into the conversation in order to lower the temperature.

'But Bertie', Elizabeth protested, 'do you mean that you believe that John has a private atom-proof shelter at Lambourne—with stores of atom-proof food, atom-proof air, water . . . ?'

---

[1] Later, in the case of the Vietnam war, the situation was unfortunately similar. We agreed with Bertie in being firmly opposed to U.S. policy, but not on the same grounds. Our view was again based on the maxim: When in doubt, do not spend £30 million a day on killing people.

'Yes', Bertie roared, 'of course he has!'

'But we have just been there; we have been *talking* to John . . .'

But for the moment it was no good; Bertie wouldn't budge. And then, a little later, he suddenly got worried that he had been too extreme. As we walked to their car, he apologized in the nicest possible way. He knew after all that we were very fond of John and he would not wish to hurt our feelings.

⟨⟨⟨⟨⟩⟩

In fact Bertie rang up the next day and apologized again. This was typical of his extraordinary mental magnanimity. There are very few people who can even suspect that they may have been wrong, much less explicitly acknowledge it to others. It is because this magnanimity was so characteristic of Bertie—and was so endearing—that I have recounted a piece of behaviour which might seem at first sight better left unmentioned. It seems to me, as I have already suggested, that this tendency of his to go to extremes of feeling when in the company of friends must have been a large element in his genius. One may disapprove on occasion—it may have made him unreasonable at times—but without this passionate feeling he would not have accomplished what he did. And there is the additional factor that he was often deliberately extreme when he wanted to shock people into noticing that something was amiss. He felt that the future of the human race was in the balance; the issue was too important for such neutral opinions (about means) as Elizabeth and I displayed. It was our duty to feel strongly not only about ends but *also* about means.

Besides, Bertie didn't *exactly* believe what he was saying. There was, I imagine, some sort of diffused picture in his mind of the 'rulers' of the country fixing things for their own convenience. He did not examine the details of the picture at all closely; and so he did not see that it might not fit a particular individual like John Strachey. What he saw was that the generalized picture was not altogether implausible. After all, the country did turn out to be dotted with underground Regional Seats of Government.

Another factor tending to strengthen Bertie's feeling was one which I have already touched upon and which may have derived from his having spent the first years of his life believing profoundly in an absolute distinction between good and evil—and also believing that he himself was often wicked. This early feeling for absolutes may have encouraged a tendency to over-simplify the 'means/ends' aspect of the H-bomb controversy and hence to overlook the fact that people who disagreed with him were often in complete agreement with him as to the end to be attained, and were disagreeing with him only as to what were the correct means to this end. He would assume that such people took the same view about causes and effects as he did; he would then further assume that, since their course of action would in his opinion bring about disaster, and since—he presumed—it would also in *their* opinion bring about this disaster, they must in fact wish for this disaster to occur. (As I said in Chapter Two he gave his friends the intellectual benefit of the doubt. They were either fools or knaves; and he presumed they were not fools.)

9 August 1958

To Bertie and Edith for drinks. We talk quite calmly about the H-bomb. I say I agree of course that at all costs we must make people conscious of the dangers (and therefore Bertie is right to agitate) though I feel very uncertain about the pros and cons of government policy.

Then suddenly—out of the blue—Bertie says, in a voice of fury: 'The next time you see your friend John Strachey, tell him I cannot understand why he wants Nasser to have the H-bomb.' When I protested that that was the last thing John wanted, Bertie's half-seriousness allowed him half to acknowledge that this was unfair. But the point is that he *was* serious, even if only half so. He was really angry for the moment. He was convinced that people like John are endangering the world, and he felt justified in saying so.

Then such a nice thing happened. As we got up to go Bertie took me over to a bookshelf, picked out an offprint, and said 'I don't think I've given you one of these, have I?' It was an article by Bertie called 'Voltaire's influence on me', reprinted from *Studies on Voltaire and the eighteenth century, VI,* 1958 (published by the Institut et Musée Voltaire, Geneva). I opened it at random. The first thing I saw was a paragraph on page 161. It began with the words 'Voltaire's attitude towards opinions that he deplored came to seem to me useful . . .', and ended '. . . In fact no opinion should be held with fervour. No-one holds with fervour that seven times eight is fifty-six, because it can be known that this is the case. Fervour is only necessary in commending an opinion which is doubtful or demonstrably false.'

⟨≈≈≈⟩

Bertie's remark about Nasser and the H-bomb was based on the premise that only by our joining a 'non-nuclear club' of nations could we confine the bomb to the U.S. and the U.S.S.R. and thus prevent proliferation. John Strachey's view was that it was now too late anyway to prevent proliferation by that means. I think Bertie in part accepted this; for he claimed that the non-nuclear plan would have worked two years earlier.

In thus denouncing John Strachey as a villain Bertie was able to reinforce his convictions with an armour of moral feeling. (His moral feelings were usually very strong; and one of the most irksome problems of philosophy for him was the impossibility of rationally justifying various ethical principles which he nevertheless could not accept as merely subjective—the 'wrongness' for instance, of cruelty to animals.)

This tendency to encourage his disapproval of people's opinions by regarding the people as wicked grew on Bertie as the years went by. I remember once, after he had fulminated against the Warren Report (on the Kennedy assassination) I reminded him of his brother-in-law Logan Pearsall Smith's aphorism (in *Last Words*): 'The denunciation of the young is a necessary part of the hygiene of older people, and greatly assists the circulation of their blood.' Bertie agreed, and added that there was no need to confine the denunciations to the young. During the last years

of his life he often commented—when things made his blood boil
—that this was what kept him going.

But, as is well known, the denunciations eventually went to
extremes which many people found excessive. Elizabeth and I
were reluctantly among those who felt such reservations—reluctantly because we were both so fond of Bertie that we hated
being at cross-purposes on so emotional and fundamental an
issue. Bertie's deafness, as I have explained, made it impossible
to carry on the tentative and sensitive kind of discussion which
alone can hold a balance between friends who hold opposing
views, who know that the views will probably *remain* opposed,
and who wish to remain friends. The result was that we gradually
ceased to discuss this particular issue at all and we also ceased to
discuss the related question of how bad—'extreme'—things have
got to be before one is justified in abrogating the democratic
process, which many people including ourselves regard as by
far the least dangerous form of government, despite all its faults.
It became understood—for instance when Bertie and Edith went
to prison in 1961—that we could express our admiration for their
stand and our concern for their welfare without committing ourselves to complete agreement.

We did nevertheless sometimes discuss Bertie's denunciations.
In common with many other people, Elizabeth and I were
puzzled at his being so extremely extreme, when he was so controlled and moderate in other fields. However, a partial explanation did emerge from his answers on the occasions when I asked
him for clarification. I think that what he was doing was to
phrase his denunciations in terms which could be interpreted in
two ways, one of which made the statement true but inoffensive,
while the other made the statement offensive but false. Then,
when he was asked to justify the statement he would rely upon
the interpretation which did in fact justify the statement while
leaving the other interpretation free as it were to insinuate its
falsely derogatory implications. The process is clearly illustrated,
as it happens, in the public letter which he wrote 'from Brixton
Prison'. Russell says: 'Kennedy and Khrushchev, Adenauer and
de Gaulle, Macmillan and Gaitskell, are pursuing a common aim;

the ending of human life. . . . To please these men, all the private affections, all the public hopes . . . and all that might be achieved hereafter is to be wiped out forever.'

Here, in talking about the 'common aim', Russell defended himself in the same way as he defended his claim that John Strachey had the aim of giving Nasser the H-bomb. The potentially justifiable interpretation of Russell's argument was that which claimed that the inevitable end-result—the 'aim' in this special sense—of these men's policies was the ending of human life. But this undeliberate and unrealized aim, though perhaps stupid, is not morally reprehensible. Accordingly, in order to justify the condemnation in his statement, Russell shifts to the other interpretation of 'aim': that which implies that these men had the conscious and deliberate purpose of ending human life. The same considerations—with a similar shift of interpretation—apply to the claim that everything is to be wiped out 'to please these men'. It might be true that the consequences of these men's being 'pleased' by getting their own way over policy would be to wipe out everything. But the implication is that they will be pleased in a more reprehensible way.

Of course there are two things one must not forget. In the first place, Bertie's extremism was sometimes deliberate. Not only did he use shock tactics in getting other people to react. He also, as I mentioned in Chapter II, made deliberate use of emotive language in order to 'cause others to share one's fury'. In the second place, however extreme Russell's views may have been, he never failed to match them in courage.

CHAPTER SEVEN

Plas Penrhyn

I PROPOSE now to print in chronological order some entries from my journal covering the late fifties. Many of these are very abbreviated, since I was not then thinking of making a consistently detailed record; and some of them concern unimportant everyday happenings—parties, people we met, selected bits of conversations with Bertie, and so on. Although in themselves unimportant, they will I hope give some idea of what life was like, in and around Plas Penrhyn and Portmeirion, for us and for the Russells during these years.

The frequent mention of drinks perhaps needs explaining. It happened that our usual times of meeting were at the end of the day when we would have drinks together before dinner, either at our house or at Plas Penrhyn. This was partly because Bertie's swallowing mechanism went wrong and he did not therefore treat meals as social occasions. But in addition, Bertie nearly always came to our drink parties; he enjoyed parties and he enjoyed people.

I do not pretend that the conversations in these journal entries are completely accurate, any more than are those recounted by any writer of memoirs. However, they were nearly always noted on the same day, and within an hour or so of their occurrence, either on a typewriter or (in later years) on to a tape-recorder.

Before starting on the journal, here is a brief résumé of what Russell was doing publicly at the time. In December 1954 he made his famous broadcast on 'Man's Peril from the Hydrogen Bomb'. In 1955 he was awarded the Pears Encyclopedia Prize, a cup inscribed 'Bertrand Russell illuminating a path to Peace 1955'. It was in 1955 too that Russell started the discussions with Einstein which led to the world scientists' manifesto against nuclear arms and eventually, in 1957, to the first of the Pugwash Conferences, which Russell unfortunately could not attend, though he did

attend the 1958 conference in Austria. In 1956 Russell resigned
from the International Congress of Cultural Freedom. (He had
already resigned in 1953 from the American Committee, partly
over their attitude towards the treatment of the Rosenbergs and
of Sobell.) In October 1956 there occurred the Suez misadventure
and the suppression of the Hungarian revolt. Russell condemned
both, but the former the more publicly, since the latter was already generally condemned by the Western World.

In 1957 Russell wrote his open letter, published in the *New
Statesman*, to Khrushchev, Eisenhower, Dulles, etc. Also in 1957
he received the Kalinga prize for his part in popularizing science.
In February 1958 came the public launching of the Campaign for
Nuclear Disarmament, and the first Aldermaston March, staged
by the Direct Action Committee, and then sponsored from 1959
onwards by CND itself. In 1959 Russell published *Common Sense
and Nuclear Warfare*. In 1960 he spoke at the rally in Trafalgar
Square following the Aldermaston March. In October 1960 he resigned the CND Chairmanship, and in February 1961 he presided
at the famous mass sit-down in Whitehall.

⁂

16 January 1957

Bertie and Edith for drinks, and to discuss more of my notes on
the typescript of *My Philosophical Development* . . . [Some discussion of universals, and of the relation between a true statement
and the facts it describes or helps us to deal with.]

I began to tell him how I admired the actual writing, especially
in the final chapter 'The Retreat from Pythagoras'; I read out
some bits of the passages he quotes from *Philosophical Essays*
(1910) on the Study of Mathematics, and commented on the
brilliant colour of their purple. Bertie said he really had felt a
sort of divine afflatus, starting suddenly and very intensely about
1901, when he was 29—just before he had his two-year impasse
over *Principia* and the logical/mathematical paradoxes—and then
very gradually decreasing in intensity. I was surprised that on such
a subject he had written so much purple, which was as purple
as the *Free Man's Worship*. He said that of course he does not

now write purple about the same things, but he can and does about politics or war or cruelty. And I said that even so the real afflatus had clearly gone; and he *rather* reluctantly agreed. I think he really knew I meant the inflated nonsense had gone, especially as I had just read his passage referring to the 1910 stuff (actually written in 1907): 'All this, though I still remember the pleasure of believing it, has come to seem to me largely nonsense.'

⌘

July 1955

Lunch in the garden. I said (having just been in a car driven by Clough): 'I felt that I was taking my life in my mouth.'

Bertie said: 'And I suppose you thought that every moment was your next.'

⌘

23 December 1955

Elizabeth said something at dinner yesterday about Bertie 'writing books right and left'.

Bertie: 'I don't write books right and left; I write them only left.'

Bertie's spelling test: I prophesy the unparalleled embarrassment of a battalion of harassed postillions gauging the symmetry of a potato peeled by a lovable but grisly sibyl.

⌘

18 May 1957

Bertie's 85th birthday. Party at Millbank. Freddie and Dee Wells. Alan Wood and his wife and some Russell relations. Alan Wood's biography launched.

[The Russells had a London flat in Millbank. Dee Wells later became Freddie Ayer's second wife. The biography was Alan Wood's *Bertrand Russell: The Passionate Sceptic*. Wood had already started on a study of Russell's philosophy, but both he and his wife died tragically within the year. As

Russell says in the third volume of the *Autobiography*, this
was extremely sad for him, since Alan Wood was in sympathy with his philosophy, and Bertie was very fond of
them both.]

⟨✦✦✦✦⟩

25 May 1957
Party for Bertie and Edith. John and Celia Strachey, Clough and
Amabel and many Bretts.

[The Bretts were Lionel (now Esher) the architect, and his
wife Christian, and some of their six children. Two of these,
Guy and Sebastian, when they later went to Eton, were
the only members of CND in the whole school. We took
them up at the time to see Bertie in order that he might give
them his blessing and strengthen their determination.]

⟨✦✦✦✦⟩

22 November 1957
Marghanita and John came up for drinks to meet Bertie and
Edith. Bertie said he knew more than any man alive about
minor Christian heresies. He described some fascinating and
improbable ones, but of course none of us had the knowledge
to justify looks of incredulity.

[Marghanita Laski and her husband John Howard were
staying at Portmeirion.]

⟨✦✦✦✦⟩

10 March 1958
Drinks at Bertie's. We were talking about Edith's heart attack,
and how well she is now. Bertie said it was an extraordinary thing
but when Edith was in danger his swallow became almost
normal.
  I told Bertie about the concentration camp book, and about

how it turned out that in camps where the guards were cruel and bloody-minded the prisoners were usually more healthy—presumably because they had something to fight against—than the prisoners in the 'easy' camps.

'I can quite believe that, can't you?' I said to Bertie. There was a pause.

'Well no', he said. Another pause; and then, in his most deliberate and reflective manner: 'I have been trying very hard, but I find I can't.'

[Edith Russell had a severe heart attack in June of 1957. She surprisingly soon recovered, and remained in almost perfect health thereafter. But at the time it was very worrying and frightening for Bertie. It was sometime in 1954 or 1955 that Bertie had begun to have trouble in swallowing: the series of muscular reflexes which push the food down the gullet did not work properly; and eventually Bertie was forced to live entirely off soft foods: Complan, milk, soup, carefully strained marmalade, etc.

The book I was reading was Elie A. Cohen's *Human Behaviour in the Concentration Camp*, trans. M. H. Braaksma, 1954.]

1 May 1958

Take Bertie to tea on the lawn at Portmeirion. The usual stir. Bertie said that at last he was finding his celebrity sometimes a nuisance. (He had always said that, at first, it was enjoyable, even when people turned out to be bores—as for instance on railway journeys.) Everybody feels they have a licence to come up and introduce themselves. We reminisced about our fantasy of Bertie pretending not to be himself in the train.

We talked about traditional morality. I suggested, as a definition: the good is that which people learn with difficulty; the bad is that which people learn easily. Bertie told us of Samuel Butler's definition: a thing is good if it brings pain first and pleasure afterwards; and vice versa.

[Butler's definition comes in the Note Books under the head-
ing 'Morality': 'Morality turns on whether the pleasure
precedes or follows the pain. Thus, it is immoral to get drunk
because the headache comes after the drinking, but if the
headache came first, and the drunkenness afterwards, it would
be moral to get drunk.']

⁓⁓⁓

18 May 1958
Birthday party at Plas Penrhyn. The (grand-) children there. Very
hot.

Bertie again produced Elizabeth's proof of immortality as his
own! He laughed when Elizabeth protested, and gave in at once,
quite prepared to believe his memory had appropriated the proof
—though he had forgotten her ever telling him about it.

[It was when we were driving down for dinner at Portmeirion some time in 1951 that Elizabeth told Bertie of this
proof. She first got Bertie to agree that the 'correct' judgement in any particular empirical situation is that which
embodies the most probable hypothesis given the available evidence. That being so, it is correct (as can be approxi-
mately verified from the Expectation of Life tables in
Whitaker) when someone is 40 years old for him to say he
will live for 30 more years; and when he is 80 to say he will
live for 5 years, when he is 90 for 3 years, when he is 100
for 2 years, and so on for ever. So it is always correct to say
'I shall continue to live.']

⁓⁓⁓

21 May 1958
Take Bertie and Edith to Bodnant. Beautiful day, car open;
enormous streaks of snow still lying in gullies near the top of hills.
Bertie's enjoyment of the gardens and of the whole outing is so
active that it produces a sort of chain reaction in all of us.

I told him of my impression that Lord Samuel had appropriated as his own Bertie's remark about Kant's one great advantage

over all later philosophers. My memory is that Bertie made the remark on the Brains Trust in 1945. Perhaps Samuel was there.

[Kant's one great advantage was that he did not have to spend years of his life in first mastering the works of Kant. The Gardens were the magnificent ones in the Conway Valley, belonging to Lord Aberconway.]

CVMMMV

I do not know the exact date of the next journal entry; a mouse has eaten it away. But it must have been sometime in June or July of 1958.

Took Bertie and Edith up to Brynkir Mills, and then for a drive up the Pennant Valley. Lovely warm day; car open.

We were talking about my views on testability. Bertie said I apparently thought that all statements should be testable. I protested that I had carefully left this open. All I was saying was that *if* we wanted to have a testable discussion (as opposed to an emotive/subjective one) then we must agree to use testable statements only. Bertie argued that, if you insist on testable statements only, then you are debarred from making all sorts of statements (for example, about the world before there was anyone on it) which we know to be meaningful.

I then said that this apparent disagreement came from Bertie's using 'testable' in the sense of 'verifiable' and my using it in the sense of 'confirmable'. A potentially confirmable statement is one where the probability of its being true is confirmable (or reducible) by making further sometimes indirect observations or experiments, while a verifiable statement, in Bertie's sense of 'verifiable', is one which is verifiable only if it is shown by direct observation to be certainly true.[1] If we insist on statements being verifiable in that sense, then we do exclude (from the canon of significance) a whole range of statements which, however, need not be excluded if we insist only that they be confirmable. Bertie accepted the distinction, but then said that the idea of confirmable statements was no use in history. How could I

[1] It is this definition of 'verifiable' which I was talking about in Chapter Five when discussing Russell's attitude towards the Logical Positivists.

possibly *confirm* that Julius Caesar crossed the Rubicon? I acknowledged that many supposed historical facts were difficult to confirm, since there was of course no way of making further direct
observations or further experiments. And then I was just going
to add that there are nevertheless many historical statements
which *can* be confirmed—for example, by consulting authorities
or by looking up relevant records, as with the actions of a king,
which are often well documented. But in the pause Bertie said:

'Well, I don't think one can say much for a theory of knowledge which doesn't deal with historical facts.'

'But it *does* deal with them,' I said. 'It merely tells you not to
believe a lot of what you see written in history books.'

Bertie (after a pause): 'Ooh! *who* was caught *there?*'

⸙

6 June 1958

Film people (making *The Inn of the Sixth Happiness*) give party
at Portmeirion. . . . Nice photograph of Bertie and Ingrid
Bergman talking.

⸙

8 June 1958

We give party for film people, also Bertie and Edith, and
Margaret and Guy. Bertie had just been reading Guy's book on
Beckford and was delighted with it, to Guy's delight.

[Margaret Storm Jameson, the novelist and her husband
Guy Chapman, the historian.]

⸙

The entries for July and most of August are the ones about
John Strachey's H-bomb views which have already been quoted.

26 August 1958

Take Robert Boothby up to see Russells. Boothby tells his story of
mediating the reconciliation meeting between Churchill and
Lloyd George.

We talk about freedom of speech and of thought.

'We must allow our opponents to think if they can', said Bertie.

[Bertie later published the remark about freedom of thought as one of the modern maxims in *Fact and Fiction*, 1961.]

⟨∿⟩

Christmas Eve 1958

Drinks party here. Bertie and Edith, Woodrow and Moorea, Stracheys, Angleseys, including Shirley's mother and aunt, Postans, Blacketts, Winches, Diccon and Frances, Michael Trevor, Betty, Euan, Clough and Amabel.

[This party is by no means untypical of the kind of party which seems to take place in and around Portmeirion and the Croesor valley. It must I think be something to do with the 'ambience' of Clough and Amabel Williams-Ellis themselves, which attracts interesting people. Indeed as somebody once complained, one finds an intellectual under every stone in the Croesor valley.

One day in 1950, when Elizabeth and I were first looking for a house up here for Bertie, we commented on how many nice people there were in Merioneth; and Bertie said all one had to do—as in the case of the Place de l'Opéra in Paris—was to sit in Portmeirion or the Croesor valley and eventually everybody would pass by. We planned a select House Agency to encourage intelligent and/or interesting people to come; and Bertie suggested that we should call it *Merioneth: A New Civilization? Ltd.*

The so-far unidentified people here are: Woodrow Wyatt, M.P. and his then wife Moorea (who is Jack Huntingdon's eldest daughter); Professor Mounia (Michael) Postan and his wife Cynthia; Shirley Anglesey's mother Hilda Vaughan, the novelist and widow of Charles Morgan, with her sister; the Winches are Henry the Explosion, already mentioned, and his wife Jean; Diccon and Frances are

Richard Hughes, the novelist, and his wife; Michael Trevor
Williams is the manager, and Betty Maxwell-Scott the
assistant manager, of the hotel; Euan Cooper-Willis is a
son-in-law of the Williams-Ellises.]

⟨≈≈≈⟩

January 1959
Take Bertie and Edith up to the top lake (Llyn Stulan) of the
Electricity Board's pump storage scheme at Tan-y-Grisiau.
Dramatic new mountain road. As they are still constructing the
dam and using explosives, they insisted upon us all wearing
black polythene safety helmets. Bertie has never looked funnier
—especially from behind—than with his white hair escaping in
waves from under this severe industrial helmet.

⟨≈≈≈⟩

2 February 1959
Take Guy (Chapman) up to tea at Plas Penrhyn. More gratify-
ing talk about his biography of Beckford and about the Dreyfus
Case (and his book on it). It was fascinating to have the Dreyfus
affair talked about by Bertie as something that had happened
within living memory. Bertie told us, incidentally, on the
authority of his living memory, that Disraeli's name was pro-
nounced 'Dizreeli'.

⟨≈≈≈⟩

At our party on Christmas Eve 1958, Bertie had asked Woodrow Wyatt if he knew about a man called Stuart Robertson, who
had been a well-known singer and who had proposed to Bertie
to make a semi-autobiographical television film of his life and
ideas. Woodrow Wyatt had not in fact heard of Robertson; but,
by a rather horrid coincidence, he heard of him again the next
day on his car radio: the one o'clock news announced his death.
Because of this Woodrow later thought of doing such a film
himself; and the next time he came to stay with us he proposed it

to Bertie. Bertie was pleased by the idea, especially as Woodrow thought he could probably get as much for the film as Robertson had offered. But, as can be understood, this depended on there being no other such film in existence. Throughout Woodrow's first discussions with Bertie, this was of course implicit.

However, when Woodrow went back to London and began trying to negotiate the sale and showing of the film he heard rumours that Bertie had in fact made such a film for the B.B.C. Woodrow telephoned me and asked me to find out whether this could be true. Bertie said at first that he was quite sure that he had not made such a film. And—with a half-amused but also fond expression—he took a little note-book out of an inner pocket; it was, he explained, the book in which he wrote down all that he actually earned by his own efforts. A most rewarding occupation, he said. (This was a further confirmation of how horribly insecure he had felt in the U.S. during the war. In his long life it was only recently—especially now that the years went by like weeks—that he had started to make comfortable riches out of his work. And naturally he treasured these proofs of security and success.)

The little book did in fact contain a couple of entries which could perhaps be payment for film interviews. There was a rather touching moment when he tried to remember what they had been for; he passed his hand over his brow in a gesture which one saw was not conventional but in fact a gesture to his own brain, and said—in a sort of pained despair—'I *can't* remember.'

This was sad and impressive evidence of the way in which short-term memory deteriorates with age. For Bertie's long-term memory was still as amazing as ever. In fact, on that very day he had been talking about politics in the years 1906–10, apropos of Roy Jenkins's book on the Parliament Act, and he had remembered not merely everything but also the dates of everything.

Bertie's memory—the ordered array of information in his brain—was of course phenomenal. I think it was probably a large constituent in his genius. For it worked like a fantastically efficient information-retrieval mechanism which not only preserved the information accurately but also ordered it so well that the relevant items were always quickly available in a form which was amenable to smooth and incisive expression.

But this applied only to the long-term memory. As his short-term memory got worse in later years, its vagaries became particularly sad and frustrating for him; he was very conscious of the disparity between the amount of information his brain used to be able to store away and what it could now do. I think the most upsetting thing I ever heard him say was in 1969 when he found he could not remember having recently met a certain well-known woman. 'But don't you remember meeting her at the Julian Huxleys?' said Edith. 'No', said Bertie, 'No, I don't remember; I don't remember anything. It is absolutely horrible being so *stupid*.'

It turned out eventually that Bertie had in fact made a long semi-autobiographical filmed interview with John Freeman, which was shown on B.B.C. television in March 1959. This being so, Woodrow could not of course go on with his original idea. However, he finally thought of a new plan: a series of thirteen short interviews, each on a special subject, with himself as interlocutor. Bertie liked the plan. And we arranged that when the Wyatts came to stay with us for Easter 1959 Woodrow would discuss the subjects and the specific questions he would ask Bertie. I went up to Plas Penrhyn with them for tea on Good Friday.

Woodrow, in working out the series, had included the subject of 'Unthinking or Taboo Morality'; and we very much hoped, since these interviews would be preserved for posterity, that Bertie would say what he really felt about sexual morality. It would be of great value, we felt, if he would in fact spell out as his the view that the only 'immorality' was causing pain and unhappiness. But Bertie refused. He argued that if he said what he really believed about sex (or about the United States) he would seem so disreputable, and would annoy so many moralists (and Americans) that he would diminish his influence; and he felt that in so far as he had any influence the prime need was to use it against the H-bomb. It is amusing to remember now how concerned Woodrow and I were; we really thought that it would be a long and hard task, requiring Bertie's assistance, to relax the restrictions of the traditional morality. We therefore argued with considerable force. I said that there was a conflict of interest between Bertie and Woodrow: Bertie wanted Peace; Woodrow wanted the Truth. Bertie said there was nothing more important than being alive; we said it was important to prevent people's lives from being spoilt by unnecessary guilts; and so on. But our arguments had no effect. Bertie was adamant; and, as it turns out, whether or not he was right, we were wrong.

⊂∿§§§∿⊃

4 July 1959

Drinks party. Bertie and Edith, Julian and Juliette (Huxley), Charles Laughton and Elsa Lanchester. Charles wearing an enormous fuzzy beard for Lear.

Elsa had a lot to talk to Bertie about, as Bertie had known her mother, who had been a militant advocate of women's rights. Elsa had horrible childhood memories of being dragged up and down as part of suffragette demonstrations.

⊂∿§§§∿⊃

8 September 1959

Take John Gilmour up to see Bertie to refurbish his enthusiasm.

We talked about nineteenth-century atheists, including Bertie's father, and about anti-scientists. Bertie told the story of Charles Kingsley refuting the 'inevitable laws of gravity' by pointing out that if you held a stone in your hand it would not fall to the ground. We worked it out that Kingsley was right! The laws of gravity are not inevitable, any more than other laws of nature (as opposed to principles). Bertie then produced the 'paradigm' of a scientific law: Light always travels in straight lines except when it doesn't. Bertie said, incidentally, that he had it on the authority of Gilbert Murray that William Jennings Bryan (the American politician) had used the same argument as Charles Kingsley.

[John Gilmour, the Director of the Cambridge Botanical Garden at Cambridge, was one of the founders of the

Cambridge Humanist Society. He is also a book collector, with a fine specialist collection of rationalist and free-thinking books. Some time in 1968 he bought a copy of Bertie's father's *An Analysis of Religious Belief* for £5. When he told Bertie of this, Bertie said he would have sold him his spare copy for £4. 10s. 0d.

The remark about light travelling in straight lines is probably familiar to those who already adopt the view that 'natural laws' should be thought of in many contexts as tendency statements. Incidentally, the same point is made, practically in those terms, in Stephen Toulmin's *The Philosophy of Science* (1953), p. 30.]

∽∾∾∿∽

1959–60

I told Bertie I had talked to Strawson at Oxford. Half-seriously Bertie said 'You have been consorting with the enemy! I shall never forgive you.'

[This was an echo of a conflict between P. F. (now Professor) Strawson and Russell over Russell's famous Theory of Descriptions. The theory had been put forward in 1905 ('On Denoting') and had held the field consistently until about 1950, when—as a reflection of a general turning against Russell's ideas in Oxford—Strawson published a paper in *Mind* ('On Referring') which attacked the whole basis of the theory.

Russell did not know of the paper until about 1956, when I happened to mention it to him in the course of a discussion of the reasons why his later work had not been taken sufficiently seriously. He then wrote a rejoinder ('Mr. Strawson on Referring', *Mind*, 1957, reprinted in *My Philosophical Development*). The argument is very technical in its details. But it may be worth saying briefly that the difference turned ultimately on the fact that Russell (though he was not always quite clear about this) treated his own view as a methodological recommendation about how a statement like 'the present King of France is bald' (uttered at the present time) should be described for the purposes of formal logic. He found that for these purposes such statements should be treated not as meaningless but as false. Strawson, on the other hand, felt that they should be treated as meaningless—or simply as not amenable to the true/false dichotomy. But, unfortunately, instead of treating this as a methodological recommendation appropriate to a different purpose from that of Russell, he regarded it as a bald fact about language; with the result that he claimed that Russell's view was 'unquestionably wrong' and hence that the Theory of Descriptions itself was mistaken.

My own opinion is that Strawson was at fault here. But in any case he should I think have acknowledged that Russell's position was different from what he had assumed, and hence that his own paper was to some extent beside the point.

In fact, Strawson never answered Russell's rejoinder (though he did eventually write a personal letter). Russell was somewhat resentful about this. I felt—and said so—that he was justified. So, when he talked about consorting with the enemy, it was already a sort of family joke. (I should acknowledge to the non-specialist reader that most philosophers would reject the 'methodological' approach to the whole issue. If Professor Strawson is among these, he would probably have felt that there was no point in carrying on discussion of a fundamental disagreement. Russell had, after all, prefaced his argument in his rejoinder with the words: 'I am totally unable to see any validity whatsoever in any of Mr. Strawson's arguments.')

After the publication of *Human Knowledge*, this was Russell's only foray into the technical field of philosophy, apart from the summary of his views which constituted *My Philosophical Development.*]

19 March 1960 ·

We went to Bertie and Edith for drinks on Saturday, after he had been in London for six weeks or so, dealing with the H-bomb campaign. His most interesting bit of news was his television interview with Dr. Teller, the head of the American Atomic Energy Project. (This was an interview across the Atlantic with each hearing but not seeing the other.) Bertie was extremely pleased about this, and very much on top of the world, because he felt that, on the whole, he had won.

The best part of it was, he said, the fact that Teller was frightened of him. Teller was nervous and wanted to propitiate him—partly he thought because his (Teller's) life had been lived with scientists and because he was rather on his own among the scientists in America; the great majority of them took a more radical view.

'If the man who makes the H-bomb is frightened of me! Well', said Bertie 'I feel I really must be *somebody*!'

We asked Bertie whether he had liked Teller. One can sometimes—disconcertingly—like people one has disapproved of in advance. He said he liked Harding very much—the soldier who had been Governor of Cyprus. But no, he had disliked Teller intensely. Teller, he felt, was a man who believed he was concerned with the happiness of human beings while really being concerned with his own mental security.

[This is the debate mentioned in the *Autobiography*, vol. III, p. 107. Russell confirms there his dislike of Teller. But, writing some years later, he says he came away from the B.B.C. studio feeling that he 'let down all those who agreed with my point of view by not putting up the better show that the facts of our case warranted'.]

⌒⌇⌇⌇⌇⌇⌒

2 April 1960

Bertie had been awarded a prize of about £5000 by a Danish foundation—for services to European culture. He is due to go soon to Denmark to receive the prize. (This was the Sonning Prize.)

I mentioned the prize yesterday evening and said something about how satisfactory it was—a capital sum with no income-tax to pay. Bertie added: 'And no supertax! All pure gain.' He always enjoys being encouraged by us to dwell on the sheer quantity of money he is now making. It is largely that he likes in any case to be down-to-earth and unhypocritical about any of the subjects which are conventionally coddled in euphemism; but it is also (as I have already said) partly that he was so uncomfortably poor during the war: he had never really got over the contrasted pleasure of knowing that he has as much money as he personally could want.

'When are you going?' I asked. He said they were going on the 18th. I asked how long they would be away, thinking somehow that it might be a week or more.

'Oh, about two days.' Bertie spoke rapidly—with business-like decision. 'We're just going over to pick up the money and come straight back again.'

It was such a complete deflation of pomp and ceremony that we all burst out laughing. Then Edith said he'd got to make a speech and that she was worried about what he would say. Albert Schweitzer had received the prize last year; and he'd been told that he could not mention the H-bomb in his speech. Oddly, Bertie had not been given any instructions or prohibitions. But we all felt he'd better make very sure of the money before he said anything. 'You'd better hand the cheque straight down to Edith —from the platform', Elizabeth suggested. And then we started a hilarious fantasy about Edith rushing off to the nearest bank and getting the cheque turned into cash while Bertie stalled in the first minutes of his speech, waiting to see her slip back into the hall with the money in her hand.

This was the most charming side of Bertie's humour—charming and stimulating because one knew perfectly well that in serious matters his actions were serious even though his comment might be anti-pompous.

⁕

11 April 1960

We went for drinks with Bertie and Edith on Saturday. We started talking about boasting, apropos of a Central European Jew whom I had seen recently and who had boasted, actually in a rather charming way, about the jobs he had recently been

offered. We said that it was only to be expected that intelligent
Central Europeans should sometimes need to pacify a sense of
insecurity in this way.

'But after all,' said Bertie, 'it isn't only Central Europeans who
boast. We all boast. *I* boast.' He laughed with the pleasure one
takes in confessing a sin which does not seriously lower one's
repute in other people's eyes. In fact his pleasure here was connected with our all having talked so often about our motives for
doing things that, when one of us did boast, he knew that the
others knew that he knew that his motives were probably
murky.

'It is one of my proofs of the irrationality of man', said Bertie,
'that all of us are extremely prone to boast even when we know
that we shall be thought ill of for doing so.'

I then said that this had made me notice something that I had
not clearly realized before. Quite often, when there is a slight
pause in a conversation and there may perhaps be five or six
topics which would be relevant to what has already been going
on, one's mind becomes completely blank except for that one
topic of conversation which will ultimately allow one to bring
in something which redounds to one's credit. It is not *just* that
one chooses to boast when one could easily have chosen otherwise; it is that one can't think what to say and that, unless one
chooses to open the only topic in one's consciousness, there will
be silence. Therefore, if one worries at all about keeping the
conversation going, before one knows it one is over the edge
into the middle of the boast.

Bertie quite agreed. He said there was always one particular
boast which came into his mind in such a situation, and which
blocked out everything else. This was the story about 'What I
did not say to the King'.

Today was the first time I had seen Bertie since Robin Gandy
had taken two mathematical logicians (Kreisel and Löb) to visit
him for drinks. I had had dinner with the three mathematicians
afterwards; and when I asked them how they had got on it
turned out that they had been enormously impressed. Kreisel
had said that it was astonishing how acute Russell's understanding
had seemed to be even though he had not done any work
on mathematical logic for about thirty years. It was not merely
that his brain was beautifully clear for somebody of 87; it was

beautifully clear for anybody of any age. In particular, Kreisel had told Russell about some new developments in connection with the notion of effectiveness—the one developed by Turing. Russell had clearly not been very familiar with the notion before, but he had immediately been able to follow all its complications and implications. (It was fascinating, incidentally, to find that Löb was very impressed by Russell's restraint and lack of dogmatism in the expression of his views. Here, he felt, was the purely rational man.)

I told Bertie that I had had dinner with the mathematicians, and asked him what he had thought of them. He said that he had been afraid at first that he might not enjoy their visit, because he had done no mathematical logic for so many years, and might not be able to follow their reasoning. But in fact he had found them very interesting; they knew all about what had been going on during the last forty years, and they had explained it all fascinatingly.

Then he paused, shifted slightly in his chair, looked earnestly concerned, and said:

'As a matter of fact, I would *very* much like to know what they thought of my . . . of me.'

[What Russell did not say to the King is in the *Autobiography*, vol. III, p. 26. Robin Gandy is now Reader in Mathematical Logic at Oxford. Martin Löb is Professor of Mathematical Logic at Leeds. George Kreisel is a professor at Stanford University, California. He contributed an essay on Mathematical Logic to the volume of essays entitled *Bertrand Russell: Philosopher of the Century*, edited by Ralph Schoenman.]

❦

16 May 1960

Bertie produced an explosion against Woodrow over H-bomb policy. Woodrow said something which implied that some of the scientists whom Bertie was relying on were too emotionally involved to be in fact reliable. Bertie then got very excited and said that Woodrow himself was emotionally involved; and so on.

I eventually calmed things a bit by saying that each was calling the other side's scientists black.

But what then was so disarming was that when Bertie did calm down he began to apologize indirectly. 'Whenever people get really serious they start to behave like schoolboys,' he said. He had earlier been claiming that what was wrong with the world was that everybody was stupid. 'Why can't we recognize that the behaviour of the governments towards each other is childish—schoolboy?'

Later the telephone rang, and it was Bertie saying 'Look here, I think I ought to apologize for being so rude this evening—getting so excited. I shouldn't have been so rude to one of your guests.' I said that it didn't matter in the least bit; it made it all very exciting—we enjoyed it. What would have mattered would have been if he had said to Woodrow 'You are being bribed' or 'You are dishonest'. Just to call him a scoundrel was nothing. And Bertie, accommodatingly accepting my olive branch, said: 'Yes of course; that is just common abuse; it is not slander.'

⁕

16 June 1960

Drinks with Bertie and Edith. They are off again to London on Monday. Their chief reason for going is to try and reconcile the American and Russian scientists in the Pugwash Conference, who have been writing rude letters to each other. . . . I asked whether Bertie had seen Cyrus Eaton in London when he was over a short time ago. Bertie said No; Eaton didn't like him at all.

We talked about Cyrus Eaton's unfortunate tendency, being so rich, to want to call the tune. But, we all agreed, we would do just the same thing ourselves if we had the money. Bertie said, in his best sententious parson's voice: 'Yes; we are all miserable sinners. . . .' Then, in his normal voice, 'Well, we are all *sinners* anyway.'

⁕

23 August 1961

Bertie and Edith for drinks. We had asked them so that Patrick and Pat (Blackett) could give them a marvellous photograph they had discovered of Bertie at the sit-down.

Patrick was the only person who could make Bertie hear—
very sad. Bertie heard hardly anything that I said, except when
I got up later and shouted—nothing that Pat said. Anyway he
and Patrick had a fairly satisfactorily agreeing conversation about
the stupidity of the U.S.A.'s behaviour. Pat presented the portrait
very nicely—with an obviously sincere desire to express admiration for Bertie's courage and determination, though she and
Patrick—like us—do not in fact agree with Bertie's view as to
what are the appropriate means to his end.

But for me the real pleasure of the evening was again Bertie's
agility of mind in dealing with a new idea. I had decided to try
out on him the beautiful new proof of the Euclidean theorem
about the angles at the base of an isosceles triangle. The point
about this proof is that it was devised by a computer (which had
been programmed with Euclid's axioms and with instructions
to deduce theorems of geometry therefrom) and that it had almost
certainly not been thought of by a human being: one can be fairly
sure of this, because the proof is so much more elegant in its simplicity than any other known proof that it would certainly have
been preferred if it *had* been thought of.

The Euclidean proof relies upon a construction. One has to drop
a perpendicular from the apex. It can then be shown that the two
resultant triangles are congruent, from which it follows that
the angles at the base are equal. I asked Bertie if he knew of any
proof which does not involve a construction. He said: 'No, I
don't. There is a proof by superposition, but that has never
been very satisfactory' (since it involves a procedure which is
not provided for in the axioms).

I then worked out the new proof, pointing to the corners of
an imaginary triangle in the air:

In the isosceles triangle ABC, with AB equal to AC; to prove
that the angle ABC equals the angle ACB.

In the *two* triangles ABC and ACB, AB equals AC and AC
equals AB. Given.

The included angle BAC equals (is the same as) the included
angle CAB.

Therefore the two triangles ABC and ACB are congruent;
and it follows that angle ABC equals angle ACB. Q.E.D.

Bertie's first reaction was to say 'But that isn't *fair*'. He didn't
think the proof was quite valid. Pat saw and accepted it at once.

Patrick was not impressed. He thought it was quite obvious; it was merely a case of turning the triangle over. He was impatient with the idea that one must have water-tightly rigorous abstract proof, rather than a demonstration in terms of empirically existing physical triangles.

I did the proof again; and then Bertie agreed without any fuss that the proof was valid. He also agreed that this was one up not only for the computer but also for my thesis that much human thinking is stultified by the human being's tendency to assume that there is—so to speak—one universal context, in which any given phenomenon either is one thing or several things absolutely. The computer—untrammelled by this assumption—did not hesitate to treat the triangle as one triangle for the purpose of premise and conclusion and as two triangles for other purposes within the proof.

Then Bertie said, 'Well of course! Naturally a computer would do better than a mathematician. Mathematicians are just stupid; I have always thought so.'

[Dr. Marvin L. Minsky, who programmed the machine, himself says in his paper, 'Some methods of artificial intelligence and heuristic programming' (in *Mechanization of Thought Processes*, HMSO, 1959, vol. I), that the student, unlike the machine 'feels uneasy about using the same triangle in two ways at the same time'.]

❦

19 September 1961

To Penrhyndeudraeth Station with a bottle of champagne to meet Bertie and Edith on their way home from Brixton Prison.

❦

Christmas 1961

Christmas dinner at Plas Penrhyn. The grandchildren are spending their Christmas with their grandmother, Dora. We had only Ralph Schoenman, the American secretary, and his sister, and an assistant secretary.

After lunch we began talking philosophy. (Schoenman read philosophy at Princeton, under Carl Hempel I think.) We first explored verifiability and significance, on the same lines as before with Bertie. Then solipsism and the foundations of empirical knowledge (again on the same lines as I have already outlined). Bertie was half jokingly evading the common-sense view that common-sense must be correct for many purposes. He said things like 'There is no evidence whatsoever'—hitting the arm of his chair with genuine impatience—'that the world will continue for more than five minutes.' When he said this kind of thing I would say: 'Agreed, there is perhaps no evidence in a certain sense. But I don't accept your "no evidence whatsoever".'

He also supported Schoenman, who said that the scientist's belief in the evidence of his senses was arbitrary in the sense of being quite unjustified. This, I argued, is to give the word 'arbitrary' a different meaning from its normal one. In its normal meaning there are of course some empirical judgements which are arbitrary, but also some which are not (otherwise there would be no use for the word).

I said to Bertie, 'You are behaving inconsistently. You are claiming on the one hand that there is no evidence for your empirical judgements, and that they are therefore completely arbitrary. But on the other hand you are basing all your present behaviour upon just the empirical judgements and predictions which you are talking about. You reach for your matches, you light your pipe, with the flame just by your nose, and you rely on the flame behaving in the same undangerous way as before . . . If you really believed what you said, you would have to lie supine doing nothing.'

Bertie then said, 'Oh I quite admit that I am a miserable sinner. I am continually acting against my beliefs.'

He later took the reverse line. Because I base my empirical judgements on what he considers unjustifiable assumptions, he said I was acting on faith—thinking exactly in the same way as a parson does.

I said, 'Not *exactly*, Bertie. That is too much. The same in some ways perhaps. But not exactly.'

'I can't see any difference', said Bertie. 'Pure religious thinking.'

We then shifted the ground of the argument. I said that in any

case what seemed to me a difficulty in his position was to justify
his claim that we need do more than find out how to deal with
the world successfully in accordance with our needs. Any knowledge which was sufficient for these purposes was indeed sufficient.
Why demand more? To ask for absolute certainty that the world
will continue in the future is redundant. All we need is to realize
that it is sensible at least to *treat* it as likely to continue.

Bertie objected that this was a petty idea. After all, man was
only a small speck of living matter in a small part of the universe.
To insist upon relating all one's judgements to man and man's
interests was to be a humanist. (He told a story about a Humanist
Society in America which decided not to invite him to speak
since he was interested in the stars, and ought to have been interested only in man.) Judgements as to how things should be
described from man's point of view are quite unimportant in
the cosmic framework; by contrast, judgements as to what
things are 'really' are *not* unimportant.

'But if these are not unimportant, that means they are important—but to whom or to what, if not to man?'

'Man himself is unimportant', said Bertie.

He then said it was simply a matter of temperament between
us. I was concerned with pragmatic and local interests of man,
while he was concerned with the wider issues—with the problem
of seeing things as they really are, not just as they are seen by man.
'I would tell the truth', he said, 'whatever consequences it might
have for human beings.'

As it was Christmas Day, I said, I would have let him get away
with this completely if it were not that he had managed to make
his own temperament sound so majestic and noble by comparison
with mine.

'But I *am* majestic and noble', he said.

31 January 1962
I heard today that J. B. S. Haldane had alleged that a certain
Tory politician had left school early because of a homosexual
episode.

When I told Bertie, he said:

'It's awfully annoying when our enemies commit crimes we don't disapprove of.'

[Some years later, in May 1965, there was a corollary to this. Apropos of the debate in the House of Lords over the Homosexuality Bill, Bertie asked me 'Did you feel pleased or annoyed at seeing that the four bishops who voted in the debate voted for the Bill?' I began to say that I felt pleased, and then of course I saw the point of his alternative. We laughed, and acknowledged our Rationalist prejudice—our worry when our enemies behaved so well as to gain good-will. Bertie said in fact he was on the whole pleased; provided the churches were progressive about that sort of thing, there was very little to object to in their continuing to provide comfort for the religious minded.

On the same occasion we discussed the pseudo-progres-siveness of some judge who had said, very kindly, that homosexuals should not be imprisoned but treated and cured.

'Cured?' said Bertie, 'Cured? Why should they want to be cured?'

'What we need', said Elizabeth, 'is to cure some hetero-sexuals and stop the population explosion.'

'Yes, indeed', said Bertie, 'a much less painful way than having periodic wars.']

CHAPTER EIGHT

The Nineties

I HAVE already mentioned the difficulties of communication which were caused by Bertie's deafness, and in particular by the unfortunate fact that the pitch of my voice was just wrong for him to hear me easily. The deafness gradually got worse, and eventually Bertie had to have a hearing aid. As can be imagined, hardly anyone could have been less well-equipped to make the best of such a machine. Bertie had never been able to produce the slightest interest in *any* machine, and had acquired such in-competence in these fields that I doubt if he could have used a hammer. (Remember his inability to make tea.) This total ig-norance of the mechanics of machines naturally made them for him objects of mystery—unpredictable, unmanageable, and with a nasty will of their own. He refused therefore to have any personal dealings whatsoever with his hearing aid. He would allow it to be stuck in his ear, but would take no part in its operation. And all this was made worse by the fact that a hearing aid, being so small, falls far short of perfection as an amplifier, and therefore inevitably alters the quality of most sounds, so that the user has to re-interpret them—to learn, for instance, that the sound which used to be produced by a car is now produced (say) by a kettle boiling over. The trouble is that at an advanced age such re-learning is almost impossible. And the result is not merely that the sounds remain incomprehensible, but also that the victim's sense of well-being is undermined by painful anxiety: he cannot rely upon what his hearing tells him, and he feels insecure in the same way (though of course to a lesser degree) as would a blind-folded man walking in rough country.

Fortunately for Bertie, Edith—who lacked no quality which could be of service to Bertie—had, since she was herself very deaf, become an expert with a hearing aid. Even so, it is im-possible to adjust these machines properly except on one's own

head; and if they are maladjusted they tend to emit a loud and
continuous whistle. Bertie's machine would constantly behave
in this fashion. Bertie was patient, but hopeless: when the whistle
was particularly strident he would observe: 'It seems in a bad
mood today.' But however dreadful its mood, Bertie would
never touch it. It was too unpredictable; if he *were* to touch it,
who could tell what would happen?

From about 1960 onwards, then, the quality of my communication with Bertie progressively deteriorated. (But he often got on
better with other people. It was very sad for me that my voice
was so wrongly pitched.) Of course there were good days as well
as bad days; but even on a good day it was often hopeless to
expect Bertie to 'catch' any unexpected statement. One of the
effects of deafness (upon which, as Elizabeth is also deaf, we have
become experts) is that catching what is said depends upon an
extremely rapid scanning of all the possible interpretations of an
ambiguous noise in an effort to guess what—given the context
and environment—the noise is most likely to mean. What this
means is that the deaf person applies perforce a variant of the
simplicity postulate: he is forced to assume that the most likely
meaning is the intended one, and only if this is so is his guess
correct. If it is raining and someone says 'It is raining', he will
probably 'hear' this remark. On the other hand, if it is raining
and someone says 'The clouds are precipitating', he will probably
hear a noise from which he can construct no meaning at all.

If Bertie found it difficult to hear the unexpected, much less
was he able to appreciate the nuances and varied emphases of an
argument designed to sort out disagreement. There were even
some days when it began to be embarrassing: if one is face to face
in conversation with someone it is horrid to have nothing to say
and equally horrid to have nothing to say which can be heard.
Bertie was marvellous on these occasions. Sometimes he would
say explicitly 'Well, this is a day for me to carry on a monologue';
and sometimes he would take the cue from my asking him some
question about his past life, and would then start on some of his
great wealth of beautifully told stories. (I suggested to Edith that
Bertie should record the best of these on tape. And I hope and

imagine that they will eventually become available on gramo-
phone records.)

Another consequence of Bertie's deafness was that he had lost
the stereophonic directional sense, and therefore was unable to
separate one voice from other voices, with the result that he
could not hear at all unless he was talking to one person only.
This had already been the case for some years, and it is the reason why
so many of my accounts of discussions with him are—literally—
dialogues, with no one else joining in.

This discussion of the difficulties caused by Bertie's deafness
will explain why in this chapter there is very little record of discussion of the controversies in which Russell was involved during
his nineties. These difficulties became so great that—especially
after Russell left the Labour Party—we practically gave up discussing foreign (as opposed to domestic) politics at all. But there
was no awkwardness involved in this. We shall always be heart-
feltly grateful for Bertie's and Edith's generosity in allowing it to
be tacitly understood not merely that our differences with them
were differences about means rather than about ends, but also—
and consequently—that we could without hypocrisy admire their
courage, as I have said, and be concerned for their well-being,
while reserving our judgement on the issues at stake.

At any rate, rightly or wrongly, Elizabeth and I felt that the
prime need was to preserve our friendship with Bertie. We were
perhaps the poorer for the consequent withdrawal from close
contact with him at his most active and passionate; but we would
have been poorer still had we not been able to see him at all. There
was after all so much left to enjoy. Bertie remained Bertie, often
witty, often gay, always full of warmth and welcome. I hope and
believe that, despite politics and screaming hearing-aids, he got
some comfort and pleasure from our company and affection.

⟨⟨⟨⟨⟩

There are other reasons why, in any case, it would be inappropriate to try and describe in detail the complications of Russell's
involvemen in such movements and organizations as CND and

the Committee of 100 and the Peace Foundation. In the first place, it would be impossible to give a brief and at the same time uncontroversial account of the issues involved. And it would be even more impossible for me to give an authoritative and uncontroversial assessment of Russell's actual achievements, by personal intervention with heads of state, in the international field. (But these—as recounted in the third volume of the *Autobiography* —do of course largely speak for themselves.)

In the second place, as I have already noted, Russell became progressively more extreme in his views during these last years. This is to be explained partly as a natural response to the extreme gravity of the issues involved, but partly also I think upon the lines which I worked out in Chapter Two. What happened during most of his life was that he went to extremes when in the presence of friends who, he knew, would understand that his large generalizations were subject to reservations. He was then able—when it came to practical politics—to withdraw his forces and to fall back on a less extreme but safely tenable position. But he continued to *feel* in extremes even when he was thinking in moderation. And this, I believe, was an important factor in his influence over other people. What happened in his nineties, though, was I think that the elastic which drew him back from the extreme positions began to perish. The mental effort needed to examine his position carefully—to be entirely rational—was just too tiring. The result was that, when he went to extremes, he tended to stay there. And Elizabeth and I found we could not keep him company, much as we wanted to for friendship's sake. This then is the second reason why we kept off certain subjects, and why there would in any case not be much point in my trying to reproduce such discussions as we had.

A third reason for saying little about the controversies of Russell's nineties is that, since this is not a biography but simply a portrait, the details of these controversies are to a large extent irrelevant.

I propose therefore to pick out, from quite a large amount of material covering Russell's nineties, a selection of incidents which are particularly illustrative or attractive. This all means, however, that the substance of this final chapter is much more lightweight than it would be if the present book were primarily biographical in intent.

⟨ ᘛᘚᘚᘘ ⟩

The first thing that happened in Bertie's nineties was his nine-tieth birthday. Elizabeth and I thought it might be nice to make something of it. So I got hold of Freddie Ayer, since he was the obvious person to sponsor a celebration, especially as he and Bertie approved of each other's philosophical views. And we organized a large dinner party of friends and admirers, with speeches and an enormous cake with ninety fluttering candles for whose appearance at the end of dinner the lights were dramatically lowered. It went off very well. There were about seventy people there, and speeches were made by Freddie Ayer, Julian Huxley, E. M. Forster, the Duke of Bedford, whom Bertie now met for the first time, and of course by Bertie himself.

The next day there was also a concert with speeches and pre-sentations in the Festival Hall organized by Ralph Schoenman, which concentrated more on the CND aspects of Russell's acti-vities. And the next week there was a dinner in the House of Commons organized by Fenner Brockway. Bertie sailed un-tiredly through all these events. It was impossible to believe that he was *ninety*—seventy perhaps, but not a day older.

It was of course later in this same year that Bertie became in-volved in the Cuba crisis. And it was as much as two years later again that he became involved, with just as much abundant energy, in the controversy over the Kennedy assassination and the Warren Report.

After the Cuban crisis was over, and we were discussing its dangers and dramas, Russell's verdict on his own efforts was 'I don't suppose I altered the course of events by a fraction of an inch.'

⟨ ᘛᘚᘚᘘ ⟩

5 December 1962

We were talking today, at Plas Penrhyn, about corruption in the police. One of the secretaries insisted that our police were quite as corrupt as any in the world. I queried this, while still acknowledging that I thought the police had too much power and were sometimes dangerously corrupt and also dangerously 'agin the left'. Bertie agreed with me. The evidence such as it was, he said, suggested that our police were very much less corrupt than those in most countries and in the U.S.A. particularly.

Then there was a pause in the conversation; and, just as we were about to turn to something else, Bertie said:

'All the same, I will believe anything against the police, *with or without evidence!*'

Christmas Day 1962

Lunch at Plas Penrhyn. Bertie hearing well. All the children were there.

We were able to enjoy exchanging despairing indignation at the American Arthur Sylvester's remark about news 'generated' by the American Government. News, he said, was 'a weapon in the American arsenal'. And also: 'I think the inherent right of the Government to lie to save itself when faced with nuclear disaster is basic.'

[Arthur Sylvester was Assistant Secretary of Defence. See *The Times*, 12 December 1962.]

The grandchildren usually alternated their Christmases between their grandfather in Wales and their grandmother in England. When they were at Plas Penrhyn, as this year, Edith organized an extraordinarily complete Christmas for them, with every sort of traditional appendage and with masses of beautiful and carefully chosen presents. But in fact Christmas 'dinner' even without the children was always sumptuous—very much a party.

Some time in his nineties Bertie received from an admirer in China a magnificent full-length red silk robe. Henceforth every

Christmas Day he wore this robe, with an ancestral gold watch hanging on the front like a decoration. He looked splendid.

⟨⟨⟨⟩⟩⟩

May 1964

Bertie told me yesterday that he recently received a letter from an admirer in Italy which opened: 'Egregious Sir . . .' How interesting that what is a compliment in Italy is an insult here. It nicely underlined, Bertie said, the effect of our establishment/public school system in condemning the man who fails to conform—who remains outside the herd.

We talked about the need for birth-control in the East. Bertie produced what is apparently an original poem of his:

> The world is so full of a number of people
> I'm sure we should all wish to climb up a steeple.

Later Bertie quoted Aquinas condemning loose sexual behaviour and warning that it led to 'pernicious blithesomeness'.

⟨⟨⟨⟩⟩⟩

24 May 1965

Elizabeth discovered that the grandchildren had never heard Bertie do his atheist's creed.

Bertie (intoning like a clerical foghorn),

'We do not believe in G–o–d; but we believe in the supremacy of Human–i–ty.

'We do not believe in a life after death; but we believe in immortality—through—good deeds.'

⟨⟨⟨⟩⟩⟩

20 May 1966

A typical example occurred today of Bertie's flexibility of mind. We talked about the Moors case (the man and woman who were convicted of torturing and killing a young girl) and about the way in which so many people begged the question about causation—assuming that the reading of books by de Sade, etc., was the cause of the couple's sadistic behaviour, when it might have been the other way round, or even a case of common causation.

While acknowledging this, Bertie said that on the whole he disapproved of sadistic (as opposed to straight) pornography being available. I then put the 'catharsis' view to him—the view that the availability of sadistic pornography was perhaps a positive safeguard in that it provided a harmless release for people who otherwise might be dangerous.

Bertie misheard me (though he was hearing very well on the whole), and thought, when I was putting the catharsis case, that I was saying there was actual evidence in its favour. Although he had already committed himself to the view that sadistic pornography should be discouraged, he said at once,

'Oh well, if that's true, then I don't see that there is anything against sadistic pornography. In fact, it should be encouraged....'

I then explained that I had simply been expounding the view without advocating it or claiming it to be correct, my point being that there was no decisive evidence either for this view or for the other 'corrupting' view. And Bertie at once modified his comment; but he did *not*, as so many people would have done, go back to his own favoured view. He quite accepted that neither view could be held with any confidence. And he completely agreed that, since there was no preponderating evidence either way, we should fall back upon an overriding principle—in this case the principle of free speech.

He said emphatically that he thought pornography in general should be freely available. His first experience of it himself was when he was 21 years old in Paris. A waiter in a restaurant showed him some filthy pictures. Bertie was shocked; and, although he was of course curious enough to look through the set, he had no desire to see them again.

Later we discussed the danger that people would get calloused by seeing too much sadistic pornography, and too much violence in films and on television. One possibility, suggested by Edith, was that there might be a sort of optimum level, below which people would find their impulses catharsized but above which they would be calloused.

'I think this is a real danger', said Bertie, 'people are encouraged to be cruel by getting used to the idea.'

I asked him whether he thought that most men, if given complete licence—both legal and moral—to kill, would find, once they were used to the idea, that they enjoyed it.

'Certainly they would', said Bertie.

⌒⌇⌒

1 August 1965

I took a philosopher called David Pears to see Bertie this morning. Pears is writing a 50,000-word piece on Bertie's Logical Atomism for a paperback reprint. But Bertie was too deaf to have a coherent conversation; so Pears decided not to ask him any of the detailed questions of interpretation he had in mind. (He arranged to let Bertie see the piece before final revision.)

I had that morning banged my forehead on the window frame of my car and there was still a narrow half-inch cut showing. As Bertie came back from shutting the drawing-room door, I started to make some remark about philosophy. Bertie stopped in front of me, paused, stared very closely, and said, 'I can't really concentrate on what you are saying. I'm so puzzled: I'm wondering why you shaved your forehead this morning.'

David Pears's wife, who had taken her baby for a walk in its pram while we were talking, called in for the last five minutes to be introduced, and brought the baby in. Bertie was charmingly polite; as we were finally leaving he got up, came and looked at the baby and said, 'It looks a very inquisitive baby!' The Pearses seemed to appreciate the compliment.

Then Bertie told us a story about William James. On being shown a six-months-old baby belonging to a friend, he similarly had looked at it, and admired it for a moment; and then had said, 'It seems a very *competent* baby!'

⌒⌇⌒

The preface which David Pears was writing eventually turned into a full-scale study: *Bertrand Russell and the British Tradition in Philosophy* (London, 1967):

29 January 1967

I raised again with Bertie the question of David Pears's book and his problem of interpretation. Bertie had decided that he did not want to concern himself any more with philosophy, since stopping the world from being blown up was more important. And so he did not want to read Pears's book. But I felt it was a pity that we should not perhaps try and clear up one controversial question: a difference of opinion between David Pears himself and J. O. Urmson as to what was the correct interpretation of Russell's views about existence. (See the note on pp. 24–5 of Pears's book.) Pears had sent me the relevant sheets of proofs; and I suggested to Bertie that I should bring them up for him to see. He could then tell me which of the interpretations was correct.

'It would be a great pity', I said, 'if we cannot at least take this opportunity of settling the question when we have the horse's mouth available.'

'But I might say both of them were wrong', he objected. 'I have never succeeded in getting anybody to understand precisely what I mean when I say "I see a chair".'

'How awful and frustrating!' I said. Then I asked him: 'Have you got it quite clear in your own mind?'

'Yes, perfectly clear. When I look at that chair, over there', he said pointing, 'I hold there is going on in my brain a sort of process . . .' He tailed off, and began to use his hands to gesture— to shape in outline a simulacrum of the chair he was looking at. 'There is a process which in some way outlines . . .'

'You see; you're getting quite inarticulate yourself', I said. 'Most extraordinary—you: the most articulate of people. . . . Isn't this an aspect of the correspondence theory of truth? You are suggesting that there is some actual correspondence between the structure of what is happening in your head and the structure of the chair?'

'Yes', he said, 'I hold that there is a similarity of structure between the chair and the percept which is the occasion of my perceiving the chair.'

[This philosophical position is the one which Russell adopted in *Human Knowledge* and which he had adhered to ever since. We had had arguments years before as to what one can usefully—and testably—mean by 'similarity of structure'. For me this notion is indeterminate (in the sense I have already indicated). For Russell, however, this was not so.

For him the question whether there was a causal connection between two events depended upon, and was decisively tested by, whether there was a similarity of structure.]

◈

7 February 1966

Just returned from drinks with Bertie and Edith.

We began to talk about Rhodesia and again Bertie attributed the worst possible motives to the Labour Party in general and to Harold Wilson in particular. He was very much amused by my story of meeting somebody who turned out *not* to agree that we could at least all agree that the Rhodesians were behaving thoroughly badly, quite apart from unconstitutionally. 'How very rum!' said Russell. This was one of his favourite expressions.

I asked him whether he thought that the sanctions would work; and he said he thought they might eventually work if the Government really believed in them, and if they persisted in them; 'But I don't think they do believe in them at all.'

I asked him what grounds he had for saying that.

'The knowledge of how badly they have behaved over everything else! I think that Wilson is just a scoundrel; and anybody who consents to serve in his Government is also a scoundrel.'

I wanted to look up a recent biography of Russell, which he had apparently never heard about. (He has no press-cutting agency, because it would cost him too much.) I had seen the biography in a bookshop and had decided not to buy it because I could borrow it from Bertie, if he thought it any good. But since he had never heard of it or had forgotten about it, I decided to make a note to look it up. I felt in my pockets and pulled out a notebook, and it wasn't the right one. So I felt in other pockets, looked for my diary, and so on.

'You seem very muddled about what is in your pockets. How many pockets have you got?' he asked.

I said I always had a minimum of six. I wasn't really happy unless I had seven.

'I have more pockets than that, and I know exactly what is in each of them!'

'But that's simple for you', I said, 'You've only got one suit.'
Edith joined in: 'He hasn't got one suit. He's got two suits.'
'How marvellous!' I said, 'that *is* a change.'

'Yes,' she said. 'He's got two exactly the same. It was partly because we liked the stuff so much and partly because we were in such a hurry we hadn't got time to choose anything else.'

Elizabeth pointed out that there was a hundred per cent improvement since the time when we were saying in the London flat that Bertie and Peter (Patricia, his third wife) sometimes lent to us. Elizabeth was unpacking, with Lena—their nice Irish maid—helping. Elizabeth had a pair of my trousers on her arm, and couldn't find anywhere to put them.

'Where does Lord Russell put *his* trousers?' she asked.

'He *wears* them', said Lena.

❧

7 August 1966

A lovely day, sunny but with a fresh breeze. We took Bertie and Edith for a drive, with the hood down. Bertie is never too hot. He wore an overcoat and waistcoat, and basked in the sun.

We drove up, through Portmadoc, to the Cwmystrallyn valley, and over the hills to Prenteg. As we came round the shoulder of Hebog and looked down into the Glaslyn estuary, there was the sharp peak of Cnicht facing us, looking—from our height—at its most impressive.

'I've been up Cnicht several times', said Bertie.

'What was it like?' we asked, 'And is it true—as Clough says—that you need a cushion on the top?'

'Yes; it's certainly true', said Bertie 'provided you've got a big enough bottom.'

He was very frail. There was no thought of his getting out of the car and walking a bit, even when we stopped to give the dogs a run. Shaking his head, he said: 'It is so nice to come out in the sun. I have been a prisoner for the last weeks.'

'You've been very busy, have you?' I said.

'No; it's just that I am too tired. It tires me too much to walk round my domain.'

❧

29 April 1967

Edith rang up yesterday and asked us for drinks, partly because
Bertie had that morning received his copy of the *Humanist* for
May, in which I had reviewed the first volume of his *Autobiography*. I had been enormously impressed with the book and
consequently my review was extremely complimentary. Other
reviews were also almost wholly complimentary, except of course
that of Malcolm Muggeridge, who somehow persuaded himself
that Russell was, on his own showing, a man of no soul and few
morals. (Mr. Muggeridge's review of the second volume, however, was friendly and complimentary.)

I had started my review with an interesting fact about Russell
as an author. On looking up Whitaker's catalogue of books in
print, I had found that there were a dozen or so living authors
who had perhaps a dozen or so non-fiction books to their
credit: Eysenck, Koestler, Julian Huxley, Galbraith. There had
been only one who had more than twenty. He had fifty-six; and
he of course was Bertrand Russell.

When I saw Bertie I asked him if he had liked this beginning,
about the books in print. 'Can you think of anybody else, apart
from Voltaire, who has had such a lead?' I asked.

'Yes, the Bible', he said.

'Ah, but that was written by forty-seven people', I said.

'Not at all; it was written by one God!' said Edith.

Then I pointed out that Voltaire's score of twenty-six in
Whitaker was not really valid, since most of this is in fact fiction.
Even so, I argued, perhaps Voltaire should, after all, keep his
second place in the non-fiction stakes; and I based my argument
upon a fact about public libraries which was new to Bertie. Many
county and borough councils used to be worried by the idea
that people obtain pure and unuseful pleasure at the tax-payer's
expense; so they insisted that a quarter of the public's free reading should be devoted to work—non-fiction—rather than play—
fiction. Accordingly one of each person's four tickets is blue and
is earmarked for non-fiction. This rule is seldom invoked now,
but the dichotomy remains; and, as might be expected, Voltaire's
fiction counts as culture rather than escapism—as work rather
than play—and hence as non-fiction.

When I first started as a regular provider of thrillers for the
Russells (their consumption was enormous) the rule was still

being enforced. But I was granted a special dispensation. The County Council felt that Bertrand Russell was probably sufficiently cultured already.

⟨✦✦✦⟩

June 1967

Some weeks ago I had found in the county mobile library a copy of one of the Bull-Dog Drummond books by Sapper. Bertie was delighted with it; and so I asked the librarian if there were any more available. A woman from the village heard me asking and produced next week, as a present for Bertie, a marvellous cache of about half-a-dozen.

When I took these up to Bertie we began talking about the fascination of the black/white villain/hero ethos of books of that time. Bertie himself had enjoyed Sapper as much as anybody, he said, even though he must have been *quite* grown up when the Bull-Dog Drummond books first came out.

One of the reasons why such an ethic was attractive was perhaps, we thought, that it allowed pure and unalloyed—absolute —judgements; no prissy reservations; no boring moderation; no pansy 'seeing-both-sides-of-the-question'. If a man was a coward, then we could condemn him and despise him as somebody inferior to us.

⟨✦✦✦⟩

18 May 1967

Bertie's ninety-fifth birthday. A nice celebration organized by Edith. Several people came up specially from London: Freddie Ayer with his wife Dee Wells; Julian Trevelyan the painter with his wife, also the painter, Mary Fedden (Julian is the son of Bertie's old friend Bob Trevelyan); Miles Malleson (the only near-contemporary friend); Juliette Huxley (Julian was ill); Stefan and Franciszka Themerson (owners of the Gaberbocchus Press, which published Russell's *The Good Citizen's Alphabet*); Mrs. Lloyd (with her husband) who is the daughter of Bertie's uncle Rollo, but somehow very much younger than Bertie; and a Russell relation who wrote under the name of Joan Henry.

The remainder of the party were locals: Michael and Benita Williams; Clough and Amabel Williams-Ellis; Mickie and Mary Burn.

It was a champagne party, starting at five o'clock and cleverly organized in such a way that we all moved from the drawing-room at about a quarter to six, in order that Bertie could sit down and rest. (He still found it impossible to sit down in a room in which there were women standing up.) As Bertie can never hear unless he is alone with one other person, he never heard anything throughout the party. All the same he seemed to enjoy himself and I think he was pleased that so many people had wanted to turn up.

‎⁂

19 May 1967

We asked Miles Malleson up for a drink today. There came in for a short time Donald Hall (novelist and new neighbour) just to meet Malleson and say how much he had enjoyed his work at the Players Theatre in the 20s and 30s. Malleson preened himself and said he was delighted to hear all this. 'Only this afternoon at tea', he said, 'Bertie Russell was saying that any man who pretends he does not like adulation is a liar.'

After Donald Hall had gone, we went on talking about Bertie. It was on this occasion that we had the discussion of his anti-Russian feelings in the 1920s which I mentioned in Chapter Two. But we soon got on to more relaxed and affectionate talk. Malleson described how he and his then wife (Joan Malleson, the gynaecologist) had stayed with Bertie and *his* then wife (Dora) in the West Country sometime in the 20s. Every morning Bertie would go for an hour's walk by himself, composing and thinking out his work for that day. He would then come back and write for the rest of the morning, smoothly, easily, and without a single correction. In the afternoon they would all go for a walk together to one of the nearby beaches. 'Well', said Malleson, 'Bertie would say—it was about a mile's walk to the nearest beach—he would always say: "Now, on this mile let us have a disquisition." Those were always the words. "What would you like us to talk about?" And I would say "God, or anything you like." "Very well, I will tell you what I think . . ."' It was the most stimulating two months I have ever had.

'He and Dora were deeply in love then; and John (Amberley) had just been born . . . I liked Dora very much. She was a good person; she stuck to her principles.'

He said he thought Bertie had not been fair to her. 'All the same', he said, 'I regard him as a very great man. And he's done wonderful work. But he's been wrong a great many times. The only thing I'd say in defence of that is that he's never hesitated to say what he thought without wondering whether it was going to get him into prison. Whereas all the other great men it's been my privilege to brush up against in my life on the stage and in writing plays—people like Shaw and Wells—they *always* wondered whether they were saying the popular thing.'

⁖⁖⁖⁖

11 July 1967

Drinks this evening at Plas Penrhyn. Bertie in very good form.

He asked me whether I welcomed the present sexual licence and liberty for adolescents. I said yes. He said: 'I agree entirely. There is only one danger, and that is that it seems to lead to failures in education.' What he meant, he explained, was that the people who were rebelling against authority were feeling so free both sexually and socially that they did not bother with their education. We finally agreed that this was not a case of cause and effect, but of each being an effect of the same cause—of money in the hands of teenagers.

Apropos of this, I asked him how one of his grandchildren was getting on. He didn't at first hear; and Edith said 'Oh she's been doing this and that.' Bertie caught this and said ruefully, 'Mostly *that*!' We speculated as to why, in such verbal pairs, the second is always worse than the first. Bertie then told us his story of the Cambridge don who said, 'There are reading parties and reading parties, and alas! most of them are the latter.'

⁖⁖⁖⁖

29 August 1967

We went up to Plas Penrhyn this evening to return the typescript of the third volume of the *Autobiography*, which we had not seen before, as it had been written during the last few years.

Bertie had said that he would not re-write any of it, whatever we said, or anybody said. He wanted to know whether there were any bits that were too boring. We said that there was nothing *too* boring, though the whole volume seemed to us to be much less interesting than the others, because there were no personalities, no sharp portraits.

⸎

18 May 1968

Bertie's 96th Birthday. Champagne and lots of genuine caviare, a present from Russia. Bertie is just recovering from 'flu; so there was no party, just us and Conrad and Chris Farley, Bertie's secretary and envoy. Conrad's wife stayed in London, as she is expecting a baby.

Edith had ingeniously arranged the candles on the cake as on an abacus, with a block of nine candles and then a block of six. Bertie blew out all the candles in about three puffs. When the champagne had been opened we all stood up and Conrad made a two-sentence speech . . . We all drank. Then Bertie got up and in orotund tones delivered his speech. 'I am pleased and gratified that you have so generously drunk my health in my champagne. And I am convinced that I shall feel a great deal better for it . . . I shall henceforth recommend this treatment to all doctors . . .'

When we had all sat down I reminded Bertie, apropos of his remarks about health, of an ingenious method which someone had proposed for testing the efficacy of prayer. The premise for the test is that members of royal families are prayed for more often and by more people than any other category of person. If therefore prayer were efficacious, royal personages should be significantly more long-lived than the average. And of course they are not. Conrad objected that this was not a properly controlled experiment. In the first place, there might be special circumstances which made royals liable to die earlier than other people. In the second place, there should have been an enquiry into the death rate among obscure royals for whom no prayers are said. The second point is of course valid. However, we all agreed that it was highly probable that the more prayed for (and hence the more politically important) royals would turn out to be the shorter lived, owing to the incidence of assassination.

It was sad, to find that Bertie had to be reminded of a quotation which had been a favourite of his. This was Anatole France's remark on being shown the room at Lourdes full of crutches, canes, eye-glasses, wheel-chairs, etc., left at the shrine in gratitude for, and proof of, miraculous cures. 'What? No wooden legs?' said France. Bertie's memory was curiously selective today. He recited the whole of 'There was an old lady who swallowed a fly'. But he had quite forgotten his own translation into modern English of the story of Sodom and Gomorrah, with its 'two personable young men'. On the other hand, he remembered the piece about St. Paul writing to St. Peter, and arranging to allow him ten per cent of whatever he collected.

Bertie produced two sociological queries: First, when did toastmasters first say 'Ladies and gentlemen, you may smoke'; and secondly, when did it cease to be immoral to travel on Sundays?

Conrad's already very well-packed memory produced a beautifully relevant story, about the Warden of a Cambridge college who was approached in the 90s by a travel agency wanting to arrange a Sunday excursion from London to the college. In his reply the Warden said: 'The Warden is convinced that your proposal is as unwelcome to the Almighty as it is to the Warden himself.'

[Conrad, Bertie and Peter's son, is now teaching history at Bedford College, London. He had earlier in the year brought up his wife—confusingly called Elizabeth—to see Bertie.]

∽∾∾∾∾

3 May 1968

We talked today at Bertie's about the biography by Michael Holroyd of Lytton Strachey, and also about the letter in the *T.L.S.* from various people including David Cecil and the Julian Huxleys complaining that Holroyd had been unkind in his portrait of Lady Ottoline Morrell. Bertie said he thought the letter was unfair.

I asked him who had originally produced the epigram: 'What is Mind? No matter. What is Matter? Never mind.' I had thought it was Balfour; and there is also a story that it appeared in Punch in 1855. But Bertie said his Russell grandmother had written it. She never tired of quoting it. She hated metaphysics—'especially after my father took to it and died of it.'

Later Bertie told his story about being introduced to Zena Dare (a great beauty of the stage in the 1920s) at a party, and neither of them realizing who the other was. They had a very pleasant conversation; and afterwards he said to somebody, 'She seems quite beautiful'; and she said to somebody, 'He seems quite intelligent'.

'Moore was more beautiful than you were Bertie', I said, 'Were you more intelligent?'

'He was certainly more beautiful than me', said Bertie. 'But as to intelligence I wouldn't like to say. . .'

Bertie's voice dwindled modestly. Then he went on: 'Everybody at the time thought he was the more intelligent. They were all much more impressed by him than by me. After all, Lytton put Moore first in his epitaph.'

I asked whether Moore's prestige was partly due to his diffidence.

'No', said Bertie, 'It was his vehemence.' He reproduced for us Moore's famous 'O-o-o', expressing not so much disapproval as astonishment that any friend should be capable of holding so outrageously false an opinion.

[There is a description of Moore's mastery of the accents of astonishment in J. M. Keynes's *Two Memoirs*, 'My Early Beliefs', 1949, p. 85.

The remark about the epitaph refers to Strachey's letter, printed in the *Autobiography*, (vol. I, p. 194) in which he says he will have engraved on his tombstone—

HE KNEW MOORE AND RUSSELL

and nothing more.]

Ⓒ⌇⌇⌇⌇Ⓒ

18 May 1969

Bertie's 97th birthday. Conrad and (his) Elizabeth and their baby, Mickie and Mary Burn, Chris Farley and Frank Hampl.

Mickie and Mary bring a large sheet of parchment with a com-
mendatory letter from John Stuart Mill, who was practically
Bertie's anti-godfather, and the concurring signatures of about
fifty people such as Hume, Voltaire, Spinoza, etc.

[Frank Hampl is a Czechoslovakian mathematical logician
who was sleeping in at Plas Penrhyn and acting as a most
efficient male nurse and helper.]

⚬⚬⚬⚬

29 August 1969

Took Bertie and Edith for a drive up to Tan-y-bwlch station on
the Ffestiniog narrow-gauge railway. It was very hot in the sun,
but the car was open so Bertie had his overcoat on. Although he
was a great deal better physically than last time (it seems likely
that he has been working off the side-effects of all the antibiotics) he was still very tottery. When we had got him out of
the car, on returning to Plas Penrhyn, with his feet on the ground
and standing up with his back to the wheel-chair, he wanted to
turn round so as to see the chair before getting into it. Frank
Hampl said: 'The chair's just behind you; all you've got to do is
to sit in it.' We held Bertie's shoulders. Sceptical, reluctant, he
began to sit. 'You expect me to sit down on thin air, do you?'
he said.

⚬⚬⚬⚬

This expedition to Tan-y-bwlch was the last time we took
Bertie out in the car, and I think the last time he went out at all.
His mind was working as well as ever, unless he was tired. But
he was getting more tired every day. On the occasions when we
saw him again, what was always remarkable was his great friendliness and warmth—even if it was a bit shadowy when he was
tired—and in particular his pleasure if we had something nice in
our own lives to tell him about.

As we had come to know him over the years it had become
more and more exasperating to realize how widely received was

the idea that he was a man of coldly materialist temperament and unfeeling intellect. The publication of the *Autobiography* did something to correct this impression, though even then there were people who managed to notice the few instances of Russell's 'shocking' frankness and ignore the many evidences of warm affection for his friends.

The writing of this book will have been largely wasted unless it has persuaded at least some people that Russell was not merely a genius but also a man whose temperament—whose highly charged sympathetic emotions—made him quite unusually warm, and responsive, and lovable. As far as Elizabeth and I are concerned the relationship which we had with him over twenty-five years was a marvellous gift to our lives—a bonus of pleasure and happiness beyond anything which our youthful selves could have foreseen.

Bertie Russell took an active pleasure in pleasing his friends; and he was very good at it.

Index